Florida Gardening on the Go

UNIVERSITY PRESS OF FLORIDA

Florida A&M University, Tallahassee
Florida Atlantic University, Boca Raton
Florida Gulf Coast University, Ft. Myers
Florida International University, Miami
Florida State University, Tallahassee
New College of Florida, Sarasota
University of Central Florida, Orlando
University of Florida, Gainesville
University of North Florida, Jacksonville
University of South Florida, Tampa
University of West Florida, Pensacola

Florida Gardening on the Go

Lynette L. Walther

University Press of Florida

Gainesville

Tallahassee

Tampa

Boca Raton

Pensacola

Orlando

Miami

Jacksonville

Ft. Myers

Sarasota

green tree frog

15 14 13 12 11 10   6 5 4 3 2 1

Library of Congress Cataloging-in-Publication Data

Walther, Lynette L.

Florida gardening on the go / Lynette L. Walther.

p. cm.

Includes bibliographical references and index.

ISBN 978-0-8130-3435-5 (alk. paper)

1. Gardening—Florida. 2. Plants, Ornamental—Florida. I. Title.

SB453.2.F6W34 2010

635.909759—dc22   2009036028

The University Press of Florida is the scholarly publishing agency for the State University System of Florida, comprising Florida A&M University, Florida Atlantic University, Florida Gulf Coast University, Florida International University, Florida State University, New College of Florida, University of Central Florida, University of Florida, University of North Florida, University of South Florida, and University of West Florida.

University Press of Florida

15 Northwest 15th Street

Gainesville, FL 32611-2079

http://www.upf.com

For my grandmother Reba Miley (1902–1970),
my aunt Pauline Walther (1912–1968),
and all the gardeners since who have
generously shared with me their love,
enthusiasm, and knowledge of gardening.

green darner

Contents

Florida Gardening on the Go

gray squirrel

A custom gate with a tropical theme sets the stage for this cottage's garden, with the "bananas" offering carefree contrast.

Introduction

Though it is clearly in my blood to grow things, for many years I did not garden. Certainly, I may have put out a tomato plant in the spring or kept a pot of parsley or basil by the kitchen door, but that was the extent of it. I had a family to tend to, a challenging and time-consuming job that I enjoyed, and gardening wasn't high on my list of priorities. But several years ago that abruptly and unexpectedly changed— one day I simply knew I wanted to garden. I realized that I needed to be growing things—really, that I *had* to garden.

When my family and I moved into our homestead on the St. Johns River, it came with a small grove of ancient, gnarly citrus trees of indeterminate origin but little else by way of landscaping. Beneath one window grew a formidable shrub that had a curious horizontal growth habit, almost like a bonsai or some shrub from the Orient. Its most distinguishing feature, however, was its shocking battery of three-inch, needle-sharp thorns. The property's only other ornamental plant—and I use the term loosely here—was an aptly named Spanish bayonet that stood guard at another window. Woe betide any interlopers who would dare to enter at either of these points!

For many years those wonderful old citrus trees fulfilled my horticultural needs. It was more than satisfying enough to watch them flush with deliciously fragrant blooms each spring, then set fruit, and see those tiny green pellets turn into luscious, golden orbs. But at some point, I needed more. When I once again embraced the gardener within me, the nasty thornbush and the wicked Spanish bayonet were the first to go. Since then I have gone through many more plants. Some, like those thorn-bearers, I intentionally executed. Others expired due to unrealistic expectations, and quite a few more bit the dust from neglect.

There, I said it. My neglect and/or ineptitude have killed a good deal of plants.

But there were some plants that didn't die. And believe it or not, some of those hardier ones proved to be my worst gardening nightmares, growing with giddy abandon, literally blotting out everything in their self-absorbed paths. It's the ultimate gardening trap—always beware the promise of a quick fix and the so-called invincible plant.

So yes, I have made my fair share of gardening mistakes—usually trying to grow plants where they did not belong or providing inadequate care. Even though many of those plants came to untimely ends, in the process I have learned what works and what does not. Most important, I know what works in this unique Florida climate. I have discovered how to create an aesthetically pleasing landscape that naturally blends into the environment, providing a habitat for native species. I have planned and planted to avoid the need to use pesticides and herbicides.

Like you, I am often busy. I have a full life to lead, and gardening is just one aspect of it. As with other pursuits, I know I am not in complete control. Nevertheless, it is always my hope that I strive to make the best decisions possible. I have also planned and planted my gardens with the future in mind, tailoring my plant choices and planting methods to minimize the need to fuss over them. All these choices have been determined by years of personal experimentation and research on how plants perform in the varied Florida environment.

These days I am often absent for long periods from my gardens, sometimes for months on end, during which time they must fend for themselves. In order to ensure their survival while I am away, I have engineered my gardens to not just endure benign neglect, but emerge in splendor. That is the ultimate purpose of this book—to help you make effective gardening decisions, avoid some common pitfalls, and prepare for glorious successes, but with an absolute minimum of the labor gardens typically require, because you have things to do and places to go.

So—let's get started.

1 ∾

Your Perfect Garden

Ten Good Reasons Why We Garden

Imagine your own perfect little garden. Can you visualize it? Perhaps your ideal is a riot of color by the front door, a cheery greeting to all who approach. Maybe it is a calm oasis of green in some shady corner out back, or a comfortable nook beckoning with fragrant plants and an accommodating chair. The garden of your dreams could also be one that offers a bountiful harvest of fruits and vegetables—to you or local wildlife. Whichever model you prefer, it is not too big or small, but just right. Can you see it? This is the garden you can create.

Gardens come in all sizes, shapes, and purposes, as do gardeners. Folks garden for a lot of reasons—here are the top ten.

1. Pleasure—Good-looking yards and gardens are visually pleasing, and the majority of people who garden do so to add color and vitality to their environment. A beautiful garden can actually extend living space by providing an outdoor room of sorts, and such attractive landscaping can increase property value.
2. Food—Whether the goal is for organic or simply fresher produce, growing your own fruits, vegetables, and herbs is another excellent reason to garden.
3. Exercise—One hour of light weeding can burn three hundred calories. Gardening can torch calories, strengthen bones, and provide healthy aerobic exercise.
4. Wildlife—If you build it, they will come. Providing food sources, water, and shelter is easy enough with the right plants and some simple structures. You can enhance the garden's appeal by making it an organic one. Just getting out into the garden puts one in proximity to wildlife. (See Plate 7.)

Nature Magnets

Attract wildlife naturally by offering food and habitat; for instance, cultivate red-flowered plants to attract hummingbirds or create a brush pile for rabbits.

5. Creativity—Working with the various colors, forms, and textures in a garden to create a pleasing whole is a creative endeavor. Add outdoor art to your garden and sculpt an instant gallery.

Recycling comes to the garden with a pathway edging of the finest vintage—a lineup of wine bottles driven into the soil.

6. Knowledge—Be it some sort of bond with the earth and wildlife or an expanded comprehension of nature and growth, gardening is an enlightening and educational lifelong pastime that knows no age limit or requirements of experience.
7. Connections—Gardeners are a generous lot, and a garden can nurture new relationships. Giving or receiving produce or a cutting is heartfelt and meaningful. Planting an extra row of vegetables and sharing the crop with the hungry can connect you with your community. Gardeners love to share their knowledge and experience with others through garden clubs, plant societies, neighbors, and friends. Garden and your circle of friends will also grow.
8. Memories—Many garden due to the influence of a friend or relative. Special plants remind us of special people and can often bring back memories. Gardening is an activity that can be shared with friends and family of all ages to create new memories for new generations.
9. Competition—Garden club shows and county and state fairs, to name a few, offer gardeners a chance to exhibit their horticultural triumphs.
10. Careers—Flower and vegetable gardeners can cash in on their pastime by opening a roadside vegetable stand or selling their crops at farmers' markets. Other gardening-centered employment options could include landscaping, garden centers, and nurseries.

So the desire to garden is there. Next you should decide what you want to grow and where to plant it.

Defining Your Garden

The first step towards cultivating your dream garden is to define what type it will be. It used to be that vegetable gardens were vegetable gardens, and flower gardens were flower gardens, and the twain never met. Today, things are different—a garden is defined by the person who makes it. It might be a large and lavish landscape, or it could be a tiny corner that takes just minutes a week to tend. In some gardens, colorful and dramatic foliage takes center stage, providing year-round interest. There are many plants that can offer colors and varied textures without flowers. Or, your garden could be one without a speck of soil in it—a water garden. (See Plate 8.)

❧ QUICK TIP

Top It Off

Add a bit of sparkle or color to the garden by using antique glass electric insulators to top plant tripods.

Luckily for the gardener, Florida's climate is conducive to outdoor living for the majority of the year. Open-air rooms can include everything from all-weather kitchens complete with special cooking and refrigeration units, to hot tubs, saunas, and lap or dipping pools, and comfortable, lighted sitting areas. Add to these options special weather-resistant rugs, and you have a small sampling of the numerous comfort items that can be incorporated into landscapes. Living outside is definitely "in," and small, strategically placed gardens add to the enjoyment of such retreats.

Today's gardeners often juggle many activities—a career, a family, other pastimes and hobbies, as well as the regular requirements of daily life that can make spare time hard to come by. Thus, many gardens reflect the compromise and complexity of modern life.

Ornamental or Edible or a Combination of Both

After the long struggle between flowers and vegetables for top billing, a compromise seems finally to have been reached in gardens that seamlessly blend the two. New varieties and planting techniques allow the integration of colorful vegetables and herbs with ornamentals. Consider clouds of frilly parsley nestled among drifts of pale-pink petunias and the spiky blooms of snapdragons, or an earthen bed filled with a decorative spiral of deep burgundy Merlot leaf lettuce contrasted with green leaf lettuce, and you get the idea. Vegetable crops and even dwarf fruit trees are moving into container gardens, with new varieties bred to climb and produce crops in

Like miniature oranges, calamondin citrus trees can be grown for the ornamental value of their fruit. These small trees are also perfect for container culture.

close quarters. These combination gardens deliver both beauty and bounty in half the space. Additionally, these combo gardens reduce the time that would have been required to tend two different gardens.

∾ QUICK TIP

Mobility-impaired gardeners will appreciate gardens that include the following:

- Raised beds, no bigger than two feet by three feet in size, for easy access
- Hanging planters of herbs or vegetables
- Containers elevated on benches or decks
- A red wagon, drilled with holes for drainage, to act as a rolling planter
- Lightweight plastic or composite pots (also provide added moisture retention)
- Vertical vegetable or ornamental container plantings with a trellis or *tuteur* (a pyramid-shaped structure)
- Climbing vegetables or tall flowers for easier harvesting and cutting

There Is Always Room for a Garden

Anyone who wants to garden can find space to do so. How about a "green" roof? While the ancient concept of a thickly planted roof (that is, incidentally, gaining momentum in the green movement) may be impractical for many, other options abound. Visit any marina and look for vessels with live-aboard residents and you are certain to find thriving onboard gardens. Since plants need relatively few elements to thrive—soil, water, carbon dioxide, trace nutrients, and varying amounts of sunshine—even apartment dwellers can grow bountiful little gardens in containers. Really, anything capable of holding soil can support a garden. A few square inches of ground can sustain a luxuriant flowering vine or a variety of other plants, provided that environmental needs are met. (See Plate 20.)

Sunflower seeds have taken root and bloomed in an ornamental bed beneath a bird feeder. Sometimes the best gardens are those that occur spontaneously.

Garden Scents

Try growing plants with scented foliage for a fragrant garden; some popular types include: rosemary, lavender, lemongrass, lemon balm, mint, and scented geraniums.

One possibility for a small, simple garden is three large pots brimming with colorful annuals. The containers could be simple and inexpensive terra-cotta pots, or they might be a combination of brilliantly glazed containers chosen to color-coordinate with the blooms they hold. Locate such a garden on a tiny mulched area, use it to lead into a stairway or doorway, or place it on a sunny patio or balcony. The annuals can easily be switched out and replaced with the change of seasons, and as the blooms expire. Elevate some or all of the containers on sturdy pilings, pillars, bricks, upturned pots, or pot saucers—this will bring the display closer to eye level. A trellis and a flowering vine will bring the action up front and add depth and dimension. (See Plate 1.)

∾ QUICK TIP

Garden Glow

Illuminate the garden at night with tea or pillar candles in creative containers to hang, place on pedestals, or set about. Try these containers:

- Inexpensive milk glass vases or cups
- Wire-bail canning jars (easy to hang)
- Pillar candles wrapped with a column of vellum paper
- Glasses wrapped with leaves and tied with raffia
- Large light fixture globes to nestle among foliage

Got a hankering for a water garden, but cannot decide where to put it? Forget the backhoe, landscaping rocks, pumps, and waterfalls. Water gardens can be adapted to all budgets and locations. Indeed, something as simple as a handsomely glazed terra-cotta pot can encompass a tranquil little water garden. (See Plate 8.) Whether it's a window box, a tabletop garden, a vegetable plot, or a full-blown landscape, there are many types of gardens that can be suited to your individual needs and desires.

The key to growing a successful garden anywhere is to meet plants' basic requirements, and to do so in a manageable fashion.

Florida-Friendly Plants Make for Carefree Gardens

The gardener looking for a near-zero-maintenance garden would do well to consider native plants. Keep in mind that this is not a restrictive category: rather, it includes hundreds of varied perennials, annuals, shrubs, vines, and trees. These native species are naturally more resistant to disease and pest infestations, which eliminates the need to apply chemicals. Because native plants have evolved to cope with the environment, supplemental watering and cold protection are often unnecessary once the plants are established.

Nevertheless, the varied selection of well-mannered, nonnative plants is not to be

Native plants, such as these cycads and live oaks, are most resistant to Florida's plant diseases and pests.

ignored. Many nonnative but Florida-friendly plants thrive in our unique climate and are not invasive. In addition, the list of Florida-friendly plants is constantly expanding as new varieties are engineered or found to be suitable. Plant developers and regional test gardens are constantly evaluating new plants for our gardens. It is imperative, though, whether selecting native or well-mannered nonnative plants, to choose those suitable for your specific growing zone.

Basil Math

Multiply your basil by placing root cuttings in a container of water; it only takes a few days for roots to form, after which you can pot the new plants.

Even before you plant anything, conditions exist in your future garden which could lead to either success or failure. Recognizing and working with these conditions— such as shade or sun exposure, dry or wet areas, your growing zone, and the like—will help ensure your garden's ultimate success. Matching your plant choices with your garden conditions is vital for healthy plants. Let's look at these conditions and see how they can be used to create a thriving, low-maintenance garden.

Coontie (*Zamia floridana*) is a Florida native that grows slowly and is heat and drought tolerant.

Planning the Low-Care Garden

Location Is the First Element

Putting the right plant—whether ornamental or vegetable—in the right place is crucial for gardening success. Rather than discuss the intricacies of plant physiology and photosynthesis, suffice it to say that all vegetative matter requires varying amounts of carbon dioxide, water, soil, nutrients, and sunshine to live. While most everyone knows that shade-loving plants such as ferns cannot withstand full sunshine, some gardeners fail to consider exposure and other environmental variables when planning their new garden. While, admittedly, not all plant needs are as obvious as those of ferns, determining those of any particular plant is actually quite easy.

Begin the process by examining the conditions that exist in the garden site. Taking the time to do this before plants are selected will ultimately save time, effort, and money.

꩜ QUICK TIP

Sunshine Varies

On winter solstice, the shortest day of the year, most areas of the state (including two time zones) receive about ten hours of sunlight. By summer solstice, the longest day, this figure will have increased to roughly sixteen hours. When it comes to figuring light conditions for planting, sunshine calculations should consider these variations, along with the seasonal angle of the sun.

Will It Be Sunshine or Shade, Dry or Wet?

It is important to note the orientation of the garden site. An east-facing garden, for instance, will receive morning sunshine. Is there a tree, wall, or other structure that provides shade for a portion of the day? Calculate the hours of full sun the area receives, because some plants require a fairly exact number to thrive (this is especially true with daylight-specific vegetable varieties). Some plants will benefit from a site that receives morning sun, helping to evaporate dew from foliage, yet is one that offers shade in mid-afternoon. Countless plants fall victim to incompatible levels of sunshine or moisture due to location. Plant tags and descriptive labels offer vital information regarding sun and moisture requirements, thereby aiding plant selection and eventual placement.

If you absolutely must have a particular plant but are uncertain whether or not it will survive in your garden, leave it in its original pot so that it can be moved if necessary. Give it a week or two in the desired location before deciding.

This combination of cycads and palms creates a shady corner; little nooks like this one are easily managed and offer a touch of paradise in a small space.

⌁ QUICK TIP

Divide and Conquer

Make one faucet do double duty by installing a Y-valve. Attach a short length of hose to one outlet for filling buckets or your watering can. The other spigot will then be available for use with a sprinkler.

Here is a useful list of symptoms to diagnose location-related plant maladies: If your plants are turning pale or getting leggy as they reach for the sun, assume that they need a location with more exposure; if their leaves appear to bleach out or turn brown, then they might be getting too much sun (evidence of overexposure can also mean that a location is simply too hot for a particular plant); too much moisture will often cause foliage to turn yellow and the plant to become limp; too little and foliage may appear gray or brown and dry. Move your plants as needed until you find the perfect location. This process of sampling spots in the garden is well worth the time required. (See Plate 21.)

Few ornamental plants can tolerate full Florida sun throughout the year (remember the seasonal variations in day length). What is in summer a sunny spot may not be by winter. If there is too much exposure, consider installing a section of fencing, a trellis, a pergola, or some other structure that helps shade a garden with western exposure. Does the garden site offer filtered or dappled sun, or full shade? Again, note seasonal changes to the site as the sun rides lower in the southern horizon in the winter and tilts north in spring.

Vegetables generally need a good deal of sunshine, so you should position a vegetable garden in the sunniest spot possible. However, summer vegetable gardens will likely benefit from some afternoon shade, since the intensity and duration of summer sunshine in Florida can overwhelm plants. Because winter gardens are planted when daylight hours are shorter, though, they often do require full sun all day. If the spot in your yard that receives the most sun is paved or cannot accommodate an inground vegetable garden, it may still be able to provide space for several large planters that can be removed after crops are harvested. In the latter case, select from an ever-expanding selection of vegetable varieties designed for container growth. With either type of vegetable garden, the potential of small spaces can be maximized by planting climbing varieties of vegetables such as beans, cucumbers, peas, squash, and even small melons. Also note which varieties are day neutral or daylight neutral (D/L Neutral) for winter and cool-season growing. Those varieties will flower and produce during shorter days and longer ones.

ꙮ QUICK TIP

Recycling Terra-Cotta Pots
- Use a fractured pot as a plant stand by turning it upside down
- Pieces of a totally broken pot can be used to pave garden paths or set into concrete paths
- In many cases the pot can be repaired: clean pieces thoroughly and use an epoxy glue for reassembly

Dry shade under the complete coverage of large trees or structures is just as hostile an environment as one without shade. Is the garden plot under a structure or a tree that restricts rainfall or other natural moisture from reaching the plants? Any site where nothing grows naturally—not even a coarse weed—is probably unsuitable for gardening, likely to grow only frustrations. One solution might be to prune back or thin out trees so that more sunshine and moisture reach the site. But it would probably be more advisable to simply mulch the area and forget about trying to garden there.

(However, as an aside, there is one plant that could triumph in this situation: sansevieria. These tough succulent plants, commonly known as snake plants or mother-in-law's tongue, thrive in dry shade, and there are dozens of varieties from which to choose. Be sure to avoid invasive species such as *Sansevieria hyacinthoides*, common name bowstring hemp.)

Is the garden site located in a depression that remains moist throughout the year? A soggy site requires plants suited for the conditions; likely candidates are certain ferns, papyrus, Louisiana iris, or perhaps *Crinum americanum*. It could also be the perfect place to establish a garden pond, although a raised bed could be a good choice for such sites to help with drainage issues.

Oftentimes the upper layer of soil can hide secrets that impact plant growth. Most of the state has a sand-based soil. Sandy soil offers excellent drainage, but has poor water-holding capabilities. Further, areas of deep, dry sand are often nutrient-deficient. In some areas an underlayer of clay or marly soil acts as a water barrier, leading to drainage issues.

Even small yards have microclimates—that is, areas that remain hotter or colder longer than do their surroundings. Locate such areas and either use them to your advantage or avoid them.

All of the aforementioned factors should influence your plant selections. The result of location-based planting is a healthy garden, one in which plants are not stressed by environmental conditions and are therefore more resistant to diseases and pests. And happy plants mean a happy gardener.

Know Your Zone

Florida is divided into several growing zones that include tropical and subtropical climate conditions. Therefore, plants suitable for or native to Zone 10 (southern portions of the state) might not grow successfully in parts of Zone 8 (Panhandle region) without cold protection.

The USDA growing zone designation is based on the hardiness of plants in a given region, with the "A" designation indicating the colder portion of a particular zone, the "B" the warmer.

These zone designations do not, however, address the issue of heat, which can also negatively impact many plants. The American Horticultural Society has stepped up to identify heat zones for the entire United States. Heat-hardiness zones are areas in which specific plants can survive, and they indicate the average number of days with temperatures over 86 degrees Fahrenheit that occur each year. Heat zones do not account for humidity or drought, but any given year may bring both to Florida gardens, along with plenty of days with 86-degrees-Fahrenheit-plus temperatures.

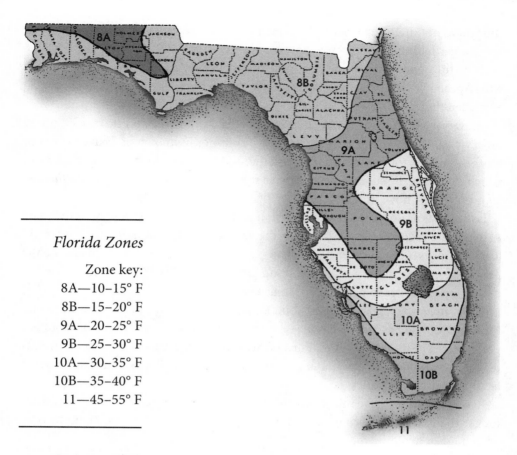

Florida Zones

Zone key:
8A—10–15° F
8B—15–20° F
9A—20–25° F
9B—25–30° F
10A—30–35° F
10B—35–40° F
11—45–55° F

While cold hardiness is an important factor in plant survival, heat, humidity, and drought add to the extreme conditions that plants must endure. Curiously, the issue of heat is where our state does a flip-flop, primarily due to the temperature-moderating influence of the Gulf Stream, which flows close to the state at its southern end, then veers away from the east coast around Cape Canaveral. It might be expected that southern portions of the state would normally be warmer than those farther north. They are in the winter months, but not in summer. Confusing?

Essentially, what this means to the gardener is that not only is Miami warmer in the winter than Florida cities farther north, but it is also usually cooler in the summer. It also rains more reliably during the hottest months in the southern portions of the state. As early as the late 1800s, gardeners such as Henry Nehrling were aware of the impact the Gulf Stream, that great ocean-bound river, "a thousand times the volume of the Mississippi, 30 miles wide and 2,000 feet deep, with the velocity of fully five miles an hour, the year round," has on our climate. Combine the effect of this phenomenon with the influence of the Atlantic Ocean and, to a lesser extent, the Gulf of Mexico, and what you have is a peninsula that dances to the tune of water. These massive bodies of water, just like their smaller brethren, lakes and rivers, greatly influence air temperatures and weather patterns. For example, the St. Johns River, which flows south to north, brings a measure of cold protection to areas along its banks far to the north. Of course, other factors like droughts and torrential rains continue to occur with little predictability, and climate change may adversely or positively affect our weather in the years to come.

If you have ever been tempted by a mail-order catalog's description of a plant that you have never seen growing in your area—yet which the catalog describes as suitable for Zones 4–9—beware. For one thing, few plants can actually tolerate such a wide temperature range. And if the plant in question does in fact manage to thrive in all those zones, it could very well be some sort of incredibly invasive plant you would be plagued by. Most often, however, the Zone 9 inclusion really pertains to a western Zone 9 where drought is more of an issue than are heat and humidity.

∿ QUICK TIP

Dryer Sheets Aren't Just for Laundry

Dryer sheets can be helpful in the garden too—try using them for the following:
- Cover holes in the bottom of pots or containers
- Cut into strips to use as handy plant ties
- Fashion a bug-repellent "flower" by running a line of stitching across a new dryer sheet. Pull on the thread to gather the sheet into a "flower" and sew or pin it onto your garden hat to keep gnats away.

This doesn't mean that you should avoid mail-order plant catalogs. On the contrary, many offer wonderful, unique plants seldom available at "big box" store nurseries or even some local garden centers. The best of the catalogs explain whether or not a plant listed as a Zone 9 plant is one that can be grown in the Southeast.

With the multitude of plant choices available for every garden location, the trick is to select plants based on your garden's particular environmental and aesthetic characteristics. Furthermore, a carefree garden should not be composed of plants that grow rampantly. In Florida, a large part of garden maintenance can be chalked up to containing plants that grow so quickly that they threaten to, or do, take over.

∿ QUICK TIP

Contain Those Cannas!

The genus of Cannas, of the family *Cannaceae*, are a perfect example of plants that, while simply lovely, can be absolute beasts to control once they get their feet rooted in your garden. They can "walk" over a planted bed in no time at all and are magnets for harmful insects. If you simply must have cannas, plant them in large containers to control their tendency to walk around the garden. Also, cut back stems to their base once flowers have faded. Use containers to control other attractive but aggressive plants such as plumbago or bananas, both of which can be stunning accents in the garden.

Nictotiana (*Nictotiana* spp.) is an annual that is easily grown from seed or seedlings, provides plenty of blooms for the garden, and makes an excellent cut flower.

Plant Terminology

Broadly, plant choices include annuals (also vegetables and herbs), biennials, perennials, vines, shrubs, and trees. Nearly everyone knows the difference between vines, shrubs, and trees. But for some, the distinction between annuals, biennials, and perennials might be a bit fuzzy. Here is a rundown of the terminology.

Perennials

Perennials are long-lived plants that return or continue growing through many seasons. Perennials often bloom only once or twice a year for a limited period of

Cane begonias provide blooms and dramatic foliage year-round.

time, but such varieties can be so spectacular that their flowers are worth the wait. Perennials do not have to be replaced each year, as do annuals, and the category includes varieties suited to the complete range of sun exposure. Examples include bird-of-paradise, daylilies, rosemary, and gingers.

∾ QUICK TIP

The Nick of Time

Hard-coated seeds often germinate more quickly and in greater numbers when they are cut or nicked before planting. Use nail clippers to nick the seeds' hard coating. Smaller ones can be lightly rubbed between two layers of fine sandpaper.

Annuals

Annuals are plants that grow, flower, produce seeds (or, alternatively, vegetables containing seeds) in one season, and then die. With flowering annuals, bloom time can be extended if the spent blooms are regularly removed. Some common examples include pansies, petunias, tomatoes, and basil. Most annuals prefer full sun, although many benefit from partial shade during mid-afternoon. One of the surprising perks of growing annuals is their very transience. Given the astonishing plentitude of new hybrids available, the ability to change out a color scheme of plantings as the seasons change is one of the advantages that only annuals can offer. Several plants that are considered annuals in northern locations can become perennial in Florida's mild climate; examples include coleus, impatiens, and wax begonias.

∾ QUICK TIP

Now Just a Minute . . .

It only takes a minute or two to do a daily deadheading of a pot of colorful annuals. Snip, nip, or pinch off old blooms at the stem. The payoff? Extended bloom times.

Biennials

Biennials are plants that produce only foliage in their first growing season, then flower, produce seeds, and die in their second. Examples of plants in this category include foxgloves, hollyhocks, *Lunaria* (common name money plant), and a few others. Because Florida's summers are so hot, few of these plants will survive to return for a second season, though that does not mean they cannot be grown here. It merely means that, if they want flowers, gardeners should purchase biennial bedding plants in their second season or else trick seedlings into "thinking" they have experienced two growing seasons.

Fooling Mother Nature

It is possible to grow hollyhocks, *Alcea rosea*, from seed to flower in Florida. In fact, it's easy, and only you will know that these handsome biennial favorites were hoodwinked into performing in your garden. It can be done in just three seasons—much shorter than the two years it takes northern gardeners to produce flowering hollyhocks. Don't pay attention to what it says on the seed packet about planting in the spring. The trick is to plant the seeds in the fall (around October) and winter the plants outside. The cooler temperatures work the charm. The hardy hollyhocks will breeze through the winter and then shoot skyward in the spring to bloom. This technique also works with biennials such as foxgloves (*Digitalis*) and rose campion (*Lychnis*).

Shrubs

Shrubs serve to fill that transitional middle ground between trees, structures, and annual or perennial plants in borders and beds, thereby providing symmetry, texture, and structure. Shrubs are either evergreen or deciduous, and many offer seasonal or season-long blooms, while others display colorful foliage that can set the color scheme for an ornamental border or bed. Shrubs suitable for Florida gardens can include, but are not limited to, azaleas, camellias, hibiscus, crotons, loropetalums, and roses.

Seven-sisters rose (*Rosa* spp.) is an heirloom rose that puts on quite a show in late spring.

Instant Rose Primer

For bare-root or potted roses: Dig a bushel-basket-sized hole. Place an entire Sunday newspaper in the bottom. Add a layer of rich soil or compost. Loosen the roots of the bush, plant it, fill in the hole, and water it well.

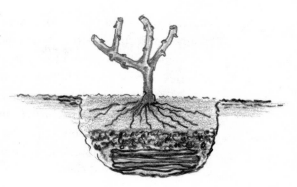

If your dream garden is a bed of roses (considered shrubs), then roses you shall have—if, that is, you have already determined that the selected site will provide good drainage and four to six hours of full sun each day, preferably with early sun to dry the foliage and some afternoon shade. In addition to their solar demands, bear in mind that roses can be the veritable gluttons of the garden, requiring more care than any other plant, especially in the case of hybrid tea roses. But even with roses, proper plant selection and placement can help reduce garden chores.

ᴓ QUICK TIP

Too Short

Once you have cut flowers, you can extend a too-short stem or strengthen a flimsy one by inserting it into a plastic drinking straw. Put it into a water-filled vessel and voila!

Instant Rose Pruning

For hybrid tea roses: In January or February prune away the top third of the plant, removing all leaves and trimming away all inwardly growing branches. Finally, replace the mulch, water the rose, and fertilize it.

Heirloom or old garden roses are often resistant to insects and diseases that commonly attack roses such as hybrid teas. The tradeoff may be reduced bloom times, but often the flowers are more fragrant than those of the fussier hybrids. Old rose varieties such as 'Louis Philippe', 'Mrs. B. R. Cant', 'Martha's Vineyard', or 'Zephirine Drouhin' will reliably bloom in waves throughout the year. (See Plate 2.) They may not produce long-stemmed rosebuds like those at the florist or like those of many of the hybrid tea roses, but they offer spectacular color and mounds of blooms with little fuss. New developments have produced roses such as those in the Knockout®, Oso Easy®, or Easy Elegance® series, which have repeat bloom periods and are resistant to diseases such as black spot.

Vines

Vines perform an important function by adding height to the garden, covering arbors and trellises, and softening the hard corners of structures. Plus, they often bring color and texture to eye level with seasonal or all-season blooms and/or colorful foliage. Perennial vines can be either deciduous or evergreen. Use either annual or perennial vines to screen unsightly views or conceal unattractive buildings and fencing. (See Plate 14.)

In general, plan on using perennials, vines, shrubs (flowering and otherwise), and even small or dwarf ornamental or fruiting trees as the "bones" of your garden. They will be a visible element year-round and will mature with your garden. These are the plants that create the backdrop for the show which the annuals perform as the seasons change—whether those are pansies, ornamental cabbages, or kales in the winter, petunias in spring, or portulacas that will bloom right through the summer's heat and humidity.

✁ QUICK TIP

Plant Tags

Handy and inexpensive plant tags to mark seedlings in flats or in the ground can be fashioned from margarine, yogurt, sour cream, or bleach containers cut into strips about one inch wide by three inches long. Also, you can recycle vinyl or aluminum mini-blinds by cutting blades into three-inch lengths to use as long-lasting tags. Use a permanent marker or contractor's pencil to mark varieties.

A balanced mix of annuals, perennials, vines, shrubs, and perhaps small or dwarf trees is essential for a garden capable of sustaining year-round interest. Additionally, any border or bed design will benefit from some sort of garden structure—a sculpture, a trellis or bench, a decorative gate or length of fence, even a substantial planter. Structures can provide contrasting texture and color and often supply vertical interest. Consider using a special urn or a colorfully glazed terra-cotta pot to feature annual plantings; this will allow them to be grouped for maximum impact and elevated above the foliage of other plants. Plus, annuals will be easy to pop in and replace as they fade. (See Plate 1.)

(See Plate 1.)

ᘯ QUICK TIP

Geraniums—Show No Mercy

Keep geraniums, *Pelargonium*, blooming and healthy by snipping or snapping off blooms as they begin to fade. The same goes for any leaves that are dried or show spots or discolorations. Be ruthless when it comes to trimming for pretty and healthy geraniums.

Whatever types of plants you plan to use, carefully study their labels before buying. Enlist the help of knowledgeable employees of a local independent nursery or your county Extension office when selecting plants for your particular garden site and zone—plants can be a substantial investment, and you want them to thrive, so be sure to select the right plant for the right place. All plants are native somewhere. Anyone who has grown an orchid knows how important it is to provide an environment which simulates the native one as closely as possible. The same principle applies to all plants.

Real Gardeners Plant Seeds

Growing from seed offers nearly limitless choices. Start seeds in flats, and when the first true leaves have formed, transplant them into cell-packs to enable good root development.

One more point is worth remembering: Not all plants will survive in your garden, no matter what you do for them. Consider every garden success or failure a learning opportunity. It is inevitable that annuals and biennials die after they have produced seed, regardless of your diligence in removing spent blooms; indeed, even some perennials are designated as short-lived perennials. Other plants are simply not suitable for Florida gardens and will not fare well.

Take tulips as an example. Although these bulbs can be "forced" to grow in Florida gardens, it is certain that they will not rebloom next year as they will do in northern gardens. But don't let this limitation prevent you from growing a pot of flowering tulips if that is what you desire. Or choose some of the narcissus varieties suitable for the Deep South. Most important, don't let the failure of a few plants discourage your overall gardening goals.

Beware the Rampant Plants

While on the one hand we want our gardens to grow and prosper, care must be taken to avoid plants that grow too well. Some plants are rampant growers. Some types of vines climb beyond control, smothering everything in their path, while other plants send out runners capable of ruining a garden faster than the worst of weeds. Several kinds cast seeds willy-nilly. These overly aggressive and invasive plants usually are the hardest to extract and the most difficult to control. Some of those aggressive plants do have their place in landscapes, but only in areas where they will not conspire among themselves to rule their little world at the expense of their more mild-mannered neighbors.

Some plants are also more aggressive in certain areas of the state than they are in others. For instance, the oyster plant, *Tradescantia spathacea*, can pose a problem in the southern portions of the state but is kept in check by the cold farther north.

While it may seem counterintuitive—even counterproductive—to select only those plants that grow relatively slowly, if a low-care garden is your desire, then select slow-growing plants and avoid those quick-growing, aggressive ones at all costs. Some of the worst offenders are classified as invasive/exotic plants for having displaced and threatened native species. The resulting monocultures of the invasive species can threaten animals and ecosystems dependent upon displaced food sources. Plants such as the Cajeput tree, *Melaleuca viridiflora*, a rapidly growing tree once popular for landscaping and wetland drainage, have displaced and imperiled native species in vast portions of South Florida. Removal of the aggressive trees continues to be labor-intensive and costly.

Welcome the Well-Mannered Plants

Instead of rampantly growing plants, look for well-mannered ones that grow slowly and dependably. To achieve a balanced garden with plenty of seasonal color and interest, utilize plants with a variety of growth patterns and textures. Many of these slow growers will prosper with little care and, more important, will not wage war on the rest of the garden when your back is turned.

Because of their slow growth, however, it is a good idea to purchase such perennial plants, shrubs, and trees in the most mature state you can find and afford when

Salt and drought tolerant, sea grapes (*Coccoloba diversifolia*) are native and can be grown as shrubs or small trees, producing numerous edible fruits.

establishing or adding to a garden. Not only does this result in a nearly finished garden from the start, but you are better able to properly position the plants with less empty space.

Furthermore, close planting aids the gardener by reducing the amount of exposed soil—prime weed habitat.

❧ QUICK TIP

Separating Seedlings

To separate tiny seedlings, carefully shake the soil from their root mat. Place the plants in a shallow dish of water so their roots can be easily untangled.

When selecting annuals from the nursery, look for those that have not bloomed but have many unopened buds and deep-colored foliage. Avoid annual seedlings that are tall, stringy, and look as if they have been in their six-packs too long with mats of roots formed outside the containers.

Top Ten Warm-Weather Annuals

(Some of these plants behave as perennials in parts of the state)
Amaranth

Blanket flower

Coleus

Horsemint

Impatiens

Melampodium

Periwinkle

Portulaca

Verbena

Wax begonia

Often annuals can be grown from seed when transplants of desired varieties are unavailable. Certainly, starting from seed is a cost-saving, though not necessarily time-saving, strategy. The same can be said for many perennials as well. The variety of seeds to select from is far greater than plant selections available at most nurseries, so growing from seed can give the gardener more choices. When purchasing perennial plants, look for those with plenty of unopened buds and thick, healthy foliage, avoiding those with flimsy, elongated growth or large mats of roots poking though the bottom of the pot (this shows that the plant is pot-bound and struggling).

∾ QUICK TIP

Top Ten Cool-Weather Annuals

Calendula

Larkspur

Marigold

Nasturtium

Nicotiana

Pansy

Petunia

Poppy

Snapdragon

Sweet pea

Top Ten Perennials

Agapanthus

Agave

Begonia

Bromeliad

Bulbine

Daylily

Flax lily

Louisiana iris

Rosemary

Sage

Don't discount the important role that vines, flowering shrubs—especially those with textured or interesting and colorful foliage—and even small trees can play as you orchestrate the symphony of foliage and flower. As mentioned before, when the seasons play out, many of these shrubs and trees will form the fundamental structure of the garden, leading the eye from upright to mounding to low-growing to cascading growth forms. In addition to providing seasonal or all-season color and bloom, the various growth forms and foliage of shrubs can provide a backdrop for the annuals' show. Regular pruning keeps shrubs and vines within bounds, making for more robust, thicker plants.

When planning an ornamental garden and/or selecting plants, it is important to study the elements that go into a well-designed garden. Consider adding colorful vegetable varieties to ornamental beds that will not be treated with pesticides. Even beds consisting primarily of vegetables and herbs can become attractive additions to the home landscape if design principles are applied. As a general guideline, any ornamental planting scheme should include plants that present a pleasing combination of:

- Colors
- Textures
- Shapes
- Sizes/heights

Some of the native and Florida-friendly plants are suited for sunny areas, others for shaded ones. Some thrive in tropical areas of the state, while others are more cold hardy. Some are salt tolerant. All in all, it's quite obvious that the list of wonderful plants far outweighs the bad, but is hardly all-inclusive. Whole books have been written on most of the aforementioned plant categories. Depending on your zone designation, particular growing conditions, and personal taste, you will find favorite plants that thrive with little care, yet do not dominate.

Secrets to Success
- Amend soils with compost
- Select well-mannered plants based on *where* they will be planted: in sun or shade, in a dry or wet location
- Provide adequate moisture with soaker hoses placed *under* a thick layer of mulch
- Inspect plants regularly to head off disease and pest problems before they escalate

Some plant species, such as the sky flower vine, *Thunbergia grandiflora*, may be aggressive in southern portions of the state while in the north it will be very well behaved, even requiring cold protection at times. In a state with such distinct growing zones (some say three—north, central, and south—while others claim five, Zones 8–12), few plants will behave the same throughout. It cannot be stressed enough that a low-maintenance ornamental garden requires *well-mannered* plants. Seek local information from garden centers, nurseries, and growers whenever possible. Even then keep your fingers crossed, and be ready to yank if things get out of hand.

QUICK TIP

Tomato Cage Uses
- To mark the location of a dormant or newly planted item
- To keep pets, children, or pests from trampling tender plants
- To hold up spindly ornamentals
- To provide a climbing structure for vegetables or ornamentals in the ground or pots
- Naturally, to support tomato plants!

Committing to the Self-Sufficient Garden

Today's gardeners have access to better, larger, and more colorful plants, as well as new products, more organics than ever before, and ergonomic garden tools. Combined, these factors help dream gardens become reality—instant gratification has arrived in the garden.

Many modern gardeners are busy with a variety of activities, and in Florida especially, where many residents live only part of the year, a low- or no-maintenance garden is what many of today's gardeners want. It would of course be difficult to find a true garden able to thrive without the occasional direction of a gardener. If you've ever returned from vacation only to discover that your beloved cannas have taken over the flower bed, you know that some plants aren't meant to be left unchecked. Practicing a bit of preemptive control is the answer.

∾ QUICK TIP

Love 'em and Leave 'em

Going away for a while? The University of Florida Extension Bulletin FCS 3154 has tips for snowbirds or anyone else preparing their home and garden for an extended absence. The article "How to Close Your Home" can also be found online at http://edis.ifas.ufl.edu/HE887.

If your garden is to be temporarily left to its own devices, there are ways to minimize the chances of trouble arising. First and foremost, it pays to plan a garden that is at least somewhat self-sustaining. Using well-mannered plants is preferable, for this precaution helps ensure that an extended absence does not allow a few plants to go wild and crowd everything else out, or that plants in containers do not dry to a crisp. It would be ideal if everyone had professional gardeners in their employ, but for the majority of us this is not the case. And for the majority of gardeners, we would not have it any other way. That does not mean, however, that we cannot devise strategies to lighten our workload.

Not everyone has the luxury of an inground or automatic irrigation system, but there is a simple, effective, and cheap way to keep plants watered without violating local water restrictions: Mulching and soaker hoses can be employed when regular rainfall falls short of expectations.

Soaker hoses use less water, delivering it right where it is needed, and when situated between a mulch layer, they function even more efficiently. In addition, these hoses do not wet foliage, thereby reducing the likelihood of disease and fungus. Finally, mulch helps to control weeds, especially when used in tandem with a barrier layer of landscape fabric.

∾ QUICK TIP

Soaker Installation

The installation of a water-saving soaker hose could not be easier. Simply lay the hose flat, threading it around the plants and through the bed. Then attach it to a regular garden hose and turn that on. Covering soaker hoses with a thick layer of organic mulch will ensure that the moisture is fully utilized by plants by preventing evaporation. Add a timer to reduce labor further.

But there's more to love about soaker hoses. When installed under a mulch layer, they provide a degree of cold protection for roots during cold weather and do the reverse when temperatures rise.

Container plantings can also be conservatively watered via drip-irrigation systems. Though a bit more complicated to install than soaker hoses, drip irrigation system components are available at many garden centers, as is home installation advice.

Generally, Florida winters tend to be dry and summers wet. Gardens left untended throughout the summer months can rely, to some extent, on rainfall, but the season's excessive heat tends to quickly dry out soil, necessitating supplemental moisture. Here again, drip irrigation and soaker hoses can come to the rescue. Inexpensive timers can limit the additional irrigation when regular rainfall is expected, while in cooler months, soaker hoses can deliver the required moisture to plants.

❧ QUICK TIP

To the Point

Recycle decorative iron drapery rods by using them as hose guides or support for climbing plants.

Container plantings can also rely on the soaker hose technique when left for periods of time, but planters should be sunk into the ground for added protection. An area that can accommodate several deep holes will be necessary. (See Plate 19.)

1. First, spread a layer of landscape barrier cloth on the area where the pots will be buried. Allow at least a foot of fabric spacing beyond and between each of the containers. The landscape cloth will prevent weed growth while allowing adjacent areas to be mowed. If necessary, weight the edges of the fabric.
2. Cut an "X" large enough to accommodate the desired pot in the landscape fabric.
3. Dig a hole as close to the size and shape of the container as possible in the exposed ground, and set the dirt aside. Soil removed from the holes will eventually refill them, and should be retained.
4. Sink the pot into the hole so that the top of the soil in the pot is at about the same level as that of the ground. Carefully fill in around the pot with some of the soil until it is snug. Repeat with any additional containers, smoothing the landscape fabric around the container so that it covers the soil outside the container.
5. When all containers have been lowered into the ground, wind a soaker hose around the outside of the rims of the containers if they are made of porous material such as terra-cotta. If they are nonporous, arrange the soaker hose so that it winds across the containers and around the plants.
6. Finally, apply a layer of mulch over the area to help conserve moisture.

Landscape Fabric Anchors

Secure edges and seams of landscape fabric with your own improvised anchors made from V-shaped twigs or aluminum fence wire (14-gauge, though coat hangers will also work) bent into a "U" shape. Use these anchors to staple the fabric into the ground.

Using this method, the containers will receive the needed water throughout your absence. An application of appropriate time-release nutrients is also suggested, especially if the period falls during the warmer months (probably not necessary in winter as many plants grow slowly then). Remember to locate your container storage area somewhere with sun exposure appropriate for the plants involved.

Plants can be stored in this fashion almost indefinitely, though eventually the roots of some plants could grow through the drainage holes of their containers. Such plants would likely need to be repotted following removal.

A Word or Two on Grass

The practice of keeping a big, grassy lawn originated on baronial European estates where noblemen paid gangs of greenskeepers to tend the sward. Picture a gathering of the gentry, bedecked in finery and playing a round of croquet on the lawn, and

Reduced turf area equals less garden work, so use turf sparingly and creatively.

you get the idea. In this day and age, however, such an expanse of grass has realistically come to represent more of a liability than an asset.

Many environmentally conscious homeowners have downsized or eliminated their labor- and chemical-intensive carpets of green. Indeed, the pollution generated by lawn mowers (not to mention gasoline-powered weed wackers, edgers, and leaf blowers) is a major disincentive to nurture a great big lawn. The Environmental Protection Agency has set tighter emissions regulations for small spark-ignition engines that take effect in 2012, the goal of which is to reduce hydrocarbons and nitrogen oxides (chemical contributors to dangerous ground-level ozone and smog). In addition, the regulations seek to limit the escape of hydrocarbons that evaporate from the equipment's fuel tanks and hoses when stored. Energy-efficient lawn maintenance tools currently on the market include many powerful, rechargeable battery-operated models.

Polls suggest that the average homeowner spends about twelve minutes of every single day on lawn and garden care, with most of that time likely occupied by their lawn. Without a doubt, nothing in the home landscape is as needy as a typical grass lawn. We feed it, we weed it, we spray it with chemicals, and then we attack it with a barrage of implements to cut, edge, and generally preen it to perfection.

∾ QUICK TIP

Step Savers

Small and inexpensive, shutoff valves can be screwed in between hoses and sprinklers, saving steps to the faucet when repositioning sprinkler heads or turning off the water for soaker hoses.

Cut back on turf area, and you cut back on the labor it demands. Of course, one excellent option is simply to do away with your lawn entirely—imagine: no more mowing or agonizing about grass health. (See Plate 6.) If that's too drastic, reducing turf area to the portion used is a good choice. Unused areas could be mulched and laid with a few stepping stones for access or planted with ornamentals, edibles, ground covers, shrubs, or trees.

For most areas of turf, experts recommend cutting grass to about three inches. (Note that some grass varieties should be mowed shorter, so be sure to check with your county Extension office for specific advice.) This length helps promote a healthy root system able to withstand heat and drought better than those lawns that are "scalped." Most power mowers do a good job of pulverizing the cut grass, allowing it to fall back onto the lawn and decompose.

If a grass-catcher attachment is used, clippings can be added to the compost pile *only if* the lawn has not been treated with pesticides, herbicides, or fungicides. (Consult the seasonal calendar for time-appropriate turf grass maintenance.)

Be sure to keep the mower blade sharp. If the blade is dull, it won't cut the grass, but tear it. Tearing can lead to unevenness, grass tip yellowing, and disease susceptibility. Mower blades should be sharpened at the beginning of a season, and preferably throughout the growing season as well (since blades dull more quickly when the grass is green and lush). Periodically check for blade sharpness, particularly after cleaning the underside of the deck when you have finished mowing. A good rule of thumb is to sharpen the blade after about twenty-five hours of use. The process is easy with a metal file. Sharpen the beveled edges of the blade by passing the file over it in the same direction each time. This is most easily done with the blade removed, since the upper edge is the one that is sharpened. If you do not feel comfortable doing this, mower dealers will hone blades for a nominal fee.

In addition, keeping the underside of the mower deck clean is essential, because a clean deck allows better contact between grass and blade. This will result in a quality cut and a great-looking lawn. Furthermore, mower life is extended by the removal of grass, which, if left in place, will quicken rust development. On the topic of mower maintenance: You change the oil in your car, but do you remember to service your mower? For the average homeowner, one oil change per year is adequate, but check your maintenance manual to be sure.

Have I mentioned that gardening can be hard work? With the planning done, it's on to the next step, where the work gets your hands dirty establishing garden beds and plots for ornamentals and edibles.

Some Basics to Get Your Garden Going

Size Counts

It has been said that the best fertilizer for any garden is the gardener's shadow. Such an expression obviously implies that the gardener's dedication is vital. A daily walkthrough of the garden—even if it only takes a few minutes—can nip many problems in the bud. Discovering a pest or disease infestation early on or pulling a few weeds before they go to seed and multiply prevents little problems from becoming disasters.

Gardening can certainly be hard work, even if the garden has been carefully designed, planned, and prepared to require little care. It cannot be stated enough: "low" care is not "no" care. That said, gardeners do sometimes get carried away and make too much work for themselves. They forget to consider the tending involved. They plan big and plant big, only to be overwhelmed by the care required. Remember that it is okay to work in stages, completing little gardens that—if desired—may eventually be combined for a big impact.

To avoid this, only plant what you can and are willing to take care of. Exceeding your limits could prove disappointing and expensive if you lose plants due to neglect. Again, there is nothing wrong with establishing your garden in several steps. Start small, experience success, and then expand things as your abilities, time, and experience allow. (See Plate 16.)

Do Not Scrimp on the Soil

Considering the trouble many gardeners go to in selecting plants, it seems absurd how little attention is generally paid to the soil in which they are grown at home. We have already determined that most plants need only a few simple things in varying amounts: soil, nutrients, water, carbon dioxide, and sunshine. Since the majority of those elements are naturally occurring and diffuse, one would think no expense would be spared on a good growing medium.

  ~ QUICK TIP

Handy Bag Tie

When opening new bags of soil, mulch, or fertilizer, first slice off the top two inches of the bag, then use this tough plastic strip to tie the bag closed if needed.

An excellent growing medium can make all the difference when it comes to whether or not plants thrive—something which every gardener wants. We may indeed have some of the best air quality and superior sunshine in Florida, but the state's sandy soils are notoriously lacking in nutrients and are infamous for harboring soilborne diseases and insect pests. Thus, Florida gardeners need to augment their soil if they expect to produce thriving gardens. One of the best pieces of advice is to amend your sandy soil with compost, or else purchase the very best commercial soils available. In short, do not skimp on the dirt.

Instant One-Dollar Tuteur

Take one wire tomato cage and turn it upside down. Bend its three or four wire legs towards the center, then bind them with wire and curl the ends outward into pleasing arcs. Place on a pot or in the garden.

Gardeners can choose from an impressive selection of commercially created garden soils and container mixes today. When planting in any container, always use a fresh, high-quality potting soil. (Old, used potting soils may harbor diseases but can be added to compost piles.) Such soils offer an appropriate and balanced medium for potted plants, shrubs, or trees. They must drain efficiently to avoid soggy conditions that can smother plant roots. The mixes also should offer balanced water-holding capabilities and slow-release nutrients to help feed plants.

When purchasing soil, lift the bag. Does it feel heavy and soggy or light and fluffy? The heavy bag is probably not your best choice, as it most likely contains a good deal of sand. The lighter, fluffier bag will fill your container with a good medium that should drain well while holding some moisture.

Contrary to popular belief, lining the bottom of a pot with a layer of gravel or rocks does not help drainage; in fact, studies have shown the opposite to be true. Instead, simply fill containers with commercial potting mixes designed to provide the correct balance between moisture-holding capabilities and drainage. After that, all that's needed is to regularly monitor soil moisture by inserting a finger into the dirt—if dry, supply water.

∾ QUICK TIP

Circle of Life

For large container plantings of annuals or for plants that will be changed out frequently, a round, plastic container insert helps to cut down on needed soil and overall pot weight. The disks, which come in graduated diameters, simply block off the lower portions of containers while providing the necessary drainage.

Commercial polymer crystals can be added to container and inground plantings to help retain moisture (most can absorb and store up to four hundred times their weight in water). In addition to holding water, these crystals often absorb added nutrients, slowly releasing them over time. Corn-based moisture-holding crystals are an organic choice. Either way, such products can help offset a gardener's absence or neglect.

Every yard with the available space would benefit from a compost pile. Composting is the ultimate modern-day alchemy—it transforms kitchen, yard, and garden waste into "black gold." Furthermore, a Florida compost pile will work more quickly thanks to our mild climate. In just a few weeks, vegetable and fruit scraps, eggshells, coffee grounds, tea bags, garden trimmings, and even most weeds can be converted into usable organic matter that can boost the growing power, increase the moisture-holding potential, and combat the pests of sandy soils. Plus, it's free. A compost pile is truly recycling at its finest, nature's own biofuel.

Volumes have been written about composting. Compact compost containers and sealable tumblers are available, but making compost is hardly rocket science, and you don't actually need any special equipment to do it successfully. Basically, compost is just well-rotted things that were once living organisms. There is no special size nor shape nor recipe for a compost pile—natural bacteria and detritivores do the trick. Compost is the best soil amendment you can find, and it can actually help plants develop pest- and disease-fighting compounds. Florida gardeners should continually add compost to inground beds, because the organic medium is often burned away or oxidized by sunshine and summer heat. Mulching heavily can help slow this oxidizing process as well as add another component to the compost as it breaks down.

To establish a basic compost pile, start by placing a thick layer of newspapers, an old shower curtain, or a tarp on the area where the pile will sit. This barrier will help contain the pile and prevent the roots of nearby plants from growing up into the pile to steal nutrients. Next, lay down a layer of dried, brown leaves or pine needles covered by a layer of green, fresh materials such as fruit cores or parings, vegetable trimmings, corncobs, eggshells, or even untreated trimmed leaves and grass. Avoid adding meat scraps as these can attract scavenging animals and/or produce unpleasant odors (the same goes for fat). However, well-trimmed bones can be added, as can crab, lobster, or shrimp, as well as oyster, clam, and mussel shells. According to some studies, shellfish shells, which contain chitin, may help reduce harmful nematodes in the soil. Furthermore, all bones and shells add calcium as they degrade. Work such items deep into the pile to prevent animals from digging in the pile and scattering the contents. Cover the separate layers with a thin coat of soil or dry leaves, leaving a depression in the center of each, and water well. Strive for a ratio of about one part green or moist components to two parts brown or dry. The compost pile should start working immediately and without odor. Turn over occasionally (once a month or so) to keep materials aerated. Add new matter as desired, covering once again with dried leaves or a thin layer of soil.

❧ QUICK TIP

Thrifty Compost Sifter

You may need to strain out larger sticks and items from the compost. A handy tool for this purpose is a plastic milk crate container. Shovel compost into the crate and shake it out over a wheelbarrow or cart, then return the larger items to the pile to finish composting.

The center of the compost pile should actually heat up, which proves that it is working. Cow, horse, and chicken manure can also be added, all of which will enhance the resulting compost. Note that chicken manure is acidic and can burn plants if applied directly. A good rule of thumb is to add chicken manure to a maxi-

Establishing a new garden bed offers a good opportunity to replace sandy soil with a garden mix turned with compost.

mum of one-fifth of the total pile. Also, although many weed seeds will compost, avoid adding plants with large, hard seeds to the pile, and do not add trimmings of oleander to any compost pile (every part of it is toxic, including the smoke created by burning it). Use the compost when it attains the look of rich brown soil. Well-rotted compost can be added to the garden at any time without burning plants. It will provide a small dose of nutrients at a metered pace. More importantly, it will add water retention to sandy soils and thereby help your plants.

Of course, making compost takes time. A quicker way to provide a complex balance of soil nutrients in raised beds or small areas is simply to replace the native soil with bagged commercial garden soils. As an added benefit, this process can eliminate nematode problems for up to a year, and weed seeds, tubers, insect eggs, larvae, and disease spores will also be removed. Try this:

1. Begin by digging out the bed, removing the top two feet of sand.
2. Replace original dirt with a half-and-half combination of commercial garden soil and homemade or purchased compost. The slow nutrient release and moisture-retention capacities of compost are just what most plants want.

∾ QUICK TIP

Waste Not

Cultivate your cuttings: When trimming back leggy coleus, impatiens, pentas, and many other plants, vines, or shrubs, root the cuttings in a jar of water with a willow stem added to help speed the process.

Commercial fertilizers can provide nutrients, but even controlled-release ones do so more quickly than compost. In addition, studies have shown that commercial fertilizers often are incompatible with the mycorrhizae (a subterranean type of beneficial fungus) that exist among plants' roots. This fungus helps plants utilize nutrients in soil, a process that fertilizer often disrupts. Compost, on the other hand, enhances it. In short, compost provides the best soil amendment, and in the long run, helps grow better, stronger plants with a healthier soil system. If additional nutrients are yet needed, try a fish emulsion mixed according to directions or an organic alternative.

Different plants require a different soil pH. Testing kits are available to determine pH, and your county Extension office can help with soil sampling.

Working with Color in the Garden

It doesn't take an artist to see what looks good in a garden. Your eyes will tell you. Still, a visit to a nursery or garden center, with the bombardment of color and texture there, can blind anyone. It is all too easy and too tempting to take one of everything, resulting in a "ransom note" kind of garden without balance, focus, or impact. The best approach is to stick to no more than three colors, or a combination of shades of one color.

Certain color combinations can increase the flowers' impact, specifically the ones opposite each other on the color wheel (complementary colors). A classic combination of yellows or oranges and blues will make each color pop with more intensity than they otherwise would. (See Plates 4 and 5.) Also, avoid the common mistake of simply alternating plantings—that is, one yellow, one blue, one yellow, and so on. The impact of any floral or foliage color display will be enhanced by grouping three or more plants of one color together. The same applies to container plantings.

∿ QUICK TIP

Plant Props

One of the most useful (and simple) garden tools is a Y-shaped stick poked into the ground to support a drooping bloom stalk or spindly plant. These natural plant props virtually disappear into the landscape so that only you will know they are there. Plus, they are free!

Gardens filled with bold and colorful foliage represent a trend that delivers year-round interest without relying on flowers. Many tropical and subtropical plants are well-suited to this style of gardening. Coleus, caladiums, oyster plant (*Rhoeo*), *Cordylines*, rex begonia, crotons, bromeliads, and even ornamental grasses are all examples. (See Plate 12.)

Monochromatic color schemes, with blooms representing the different shades and tints of one color, can take the guesswork out of plant selection and provide easy, instant coordination. Color patterns can be repeated in foliage for nonstop color when nothing is blooming. Vary bloom shapes, sizes, and textures for interest and balance, or match one spectacular plant to a container and let it command attention single-handedly. Suggestions for this role include foxtail ferns, agaves, ornamental grasses, begonias, caladiums, crotons, and coleus, just to name a few.

Color in the garden does not have to originate just from plants. After all, garden ornamentation has come a long way from plastic flamingoes and garden gnomes; many of today's gardens utilize brilliantly glazed terra-cotta or lightweight fiberglass pots for strategic color impact. Structures such as arbors, fences, and painted or stained garden furniture can help establish the color scheme. Garden sculptures can range anywhere from grand, custom-made pieces to found objects with textural contrast. Wherever color is used, it can rev up or cool down the surroundings, provide a bridge between dissimilar objects or contrast or a combination thereof. Picture an Adirondack chair painted a spicy pimento color, or conversely a cooling hyacinth blue. Then, visualize what blooms and foliage could play off that accent piece. Let color sculpt your dream garden.

The Importance of Height

As important as color is, attractive gardens need more than just a pleasing blend of color. Texture from varying leaf shapes and growth habits as well as varied plant heights are two of the three integral components of a beautiful garden. Climbing plants, garden structures such as trellises, pergolas, *tuteurs*, arbors, fences, and walls, garden sculptures, and tall plants can all add height and visual focal points to a garden.

When applied appropriately, the three components of garden design (color, texture, and height) instantly transform a simple garden into a stunning one. Elevating some of the plantings closer to eye level is one way to bring height to the garden. Implementing the principle can be as easy as varying the sizes or heights of three container plantings. Try placing pots on pedestals or adding a trellis to an inground or container planting scheme. A vine-covered pergola, a birdbath, an attractive bird feeder on a pole or post, or even hanging planters can deliver visual height variation. In some cases, small shrubs, trees, topiaries, or plants groomed as standards can themselves provide the elements of height.

∿ QUICK TIP

Have a Seat

Don't forget seating in the garden—provide places to linger and enjoy the setting. A brilliantly painted garden chair (or one with colorful cushions) can add touches of color, texture, and contrast. (See Plate 17.)

Where garden space is limited, gardening vertically also maximizes efficiency. Tall plants, or those elevated closer to eye level, help enhance the viewer's enjoyment—both visually and aromatically, if they are fragrant.

Ask any vegetable gardener whether they would rather harvest a crop of bush beans or pole beans, and most would opt for the taller plant because it eliminates the need to stoop. Climbing vegetables aren't just easier to pick, they make best use of garden space as well.

Ornamental or edible, always consider adding an element of height to your garden. It not only breaks the monotony of a single planted plane, but it enhances the total garden experience.

∾ QUICK TIP

Top Ten Easiest Vegetables
Arugula
Bok choy
Beans (bush or pole)
Cucumber
Lettuce
Peas (snow or green)
Radish
Spinach
Squash (zucchini/crookneck)
Tomato

Preparing the Garden Site

It is helpful to use a garden hose or length of rope to outline the perimeter of an ornamental garden bed before beginning to dig. For geometric shapes, use short stakes and string to define the area. Also note that there is an easy way to remove grass or weeds from any future garden site: Instead of using herbicides to prep the spot, cover it with a thick layer of newspapers (printed with soy inks only). Weigh down their edges with bricks, wood, or pipe. It may not be pretty, but it works and is nontoxic. If appearance is an issue, you can spread a layer of mulch over all.
In a few weeks the underlying vegetation will die, and it can then be raked up and removed before cultivating. Also, removing the grass and weeds in this way will help ensure that you aren't just turning under more weed seeds. This process takes a bit of time, but it cannot be beat in terms of ease, effectiveness, and economy.

Another similar garden prep process involves solarization, whereby a layer of clear plastic is spread over an area, sealed around the perimeter with soil, and allowed to sit for at least a month, preferably in summer. In addition to killing weeds, this process can destroy nematodes (microscopic organisms that live in the soil and damage plant roots) and soil pathogens. After a month the soil can be amended with compost and planted.

Mulch, the Formula for Success

Though we have already touched on the topic of mulch, there is yet plenty to consider when examining this vital garden component. Florida gardens in particular benefit from the use of mulch for several reasons:

- Mulch helps reduce weeds.
- Mulch provides an insulating layer that protects from both extreme heat and cold. This property also keeps organic soil additives from oxidizing in Florida's summers.
- Mulch helps conserve soil moisture, thereby reducing watering needs.
- Mulch breaks down over time and enriches the soil with organic components.
- Mulch provides an attractive "canvas" surrounding plants with a consistent texture.

Also, mulch can be comprised of a variety of substances. Plant materials found naturally in many yards can be used to mulch beds—dried leaves, for instance, such as those from the live oak, pine needles, or even Spanish moss can be used, although some materials require special handling. For instance, large leaves must be dry and should be shredded before being used as mulch or else they could form a compact layer that would prevent rainfall or supplemental water from reaching the soil. Live oak leaves are small enough to allow water penetration, as are pine needles and Spanish moss. Freshly cut grass or other green garden trimmings should not be used as mulch, though, because their breakdown uses nitrogen, effectively stealing it from plants. Instead, add these items to the compost pile.

To be effective for weed control and moisture retention, most mulch applications should be about three inches thick. Do not mulch right up to plants, shrubs, or trees as the mulch could harbor insects or promote harmful fungus and disease.

For the best weed control, spread a layer of landscape fabric on top of the soil before mulching—this is best done before plants are added. When it comes time to plant, cut a slit or an "X" in the fabric to accommodate the plant. Then place soaker hoses on top of the landscape fabric as a simple irrigation system, finally adding mulch.

The use of cypress mulch has long been discouraged because harvest of the trees for this purpose damages wetlands. Many municipalities process yard and tree waste into free or low-cost mulch, or you could try commercially produced mulches made of pine bark or melaleuca trees.

Synthetic mulches such as shredded rubber, although long-lasting, do not provide insulation and can actually heat soils to harmful levels. Such mulches also fail to provide the soil enhancements that organic mulches or compost do. With these disadvantages in mind, use them only if necessary.

Mulch can perform many of the same tasks in containers that it does on the ground. Don't forget your containers when you mulch, because it helps prevent weeds from seeding in, cools the soil, and holds in moisture. A layer of landscape cloth cut to fit inside the container among the plants will provide excellent weed control. Further, both mulch and landscape cloth are useful in deterring squirrels or other animals from digging in containers.

Planting an Ornamental Garden

Now that you know what type of garden you want, the ground or containers are prepared, and you have the chosen plants, it's time to arrange them.

1. Though preparing a garden diagram on paper can be helpful, it really isn't necessary when it comes time to plant. Simply place the plants, still potted, in trial locations. Remember to consider the mature height of each plant, putting the tallest at the rear of the inground garden or in the center of the container garden. Remember to place foundation shrubs far enough away from structures to compensate for their mature growth dimensions while still allowing access to foundations and walls for proper air flow, maintenance, painting, and so forth. Doing this trial arrangement presents an opportunity to double-check locations before committing the plants to the ground. At this stage there is still time to move the potted plants to achieve better balance and contrast.
2. Starting with the tallest plants, size them up and dig holes large enough to accommodate their root-balls.
3. Loosen roots if possible, as this helps plants spread quickly and get established. You can use a sharp knife to slice a shallow "X" across the root-ball, or just loosen the roots with your fingers.
4. Place the plants in their holes and smooth soil around them, being careful to keep the soil level the same as it was in the pot. Planting trees, shrubs, and many other plants too deeply may limit their growth.
5. Fill in the area around the plants and water thoroughly to eliminate air pockets that could dry out the roots.
6. For extra insurance at the time of planting, apply a water-soluble root-growth enhancer diluted according to directions. Use again as required in several days. This step is well worth the minimal effort and expense required, as it ensures that plants hit the ground running and establish a strong root system. A water-soluble fertilizer or appropriately mixed fish emulsion can also be applied to the foliage and planting area to help new plants adjust and thrive.

Seed Cubes

Hard seeds, such as those of okra, will germinate better if frozen first. Drop a couple of seeds into each section of a plastic ice cube tray, then fill the cells with water and freeze. Once frozen, the ice cubes are ready to plant.

Planting a Vegetable Garden

Unlike a garden of ornamentals, a vegetable garden cannot really withstand long periods of inattention because vegetables are annuals that flower, fruit, and die in one season. Additionally, most vegetable crops need frequent monitoring for insect and disease invasions. Even so, growing vegetables does not have to consume too much time or space. Whether in small but intensively planted beds, raised beds, or containers, many vegetable varieties can produce bountiful crops with only regular watering and fertilization.

You don't need a tractor or even a tiller to prepare an inground vegetable bed.

One of the most popular vegetable crops, the tomato is also one of the easiest to grow.

Imagine alternating strips of mulched areas and cultivated vegetable rows. The gardener can use a shovel to turn the soil only in the rows that are to be planted, while the uncultivated strips need only be mulched. This system reduces the labor of cultivating and weeding, will provide moisture-saving mulched areas, and will ultimately enrich the soil. Finally, the mulched areas will also provide clean pathways that grant access to your crops. Here is how it is done:

1. Begin by mowing (if needed) the area to be planted.
2. Mark out the rows, leaving a wide grassy strip (one to two feet wide) between each row. Remove all weeds and/or sod in the rows to be planted, then turn the soil within them.
3. Amend the turned rows with compost.
4. To prepare the uncultivated parts of the garden, spread a thick layer of newspapers (soy inks only) between the turned rows right on top of the strips of mowed grass/weeds. There is no need to remove the grass in these areas, nor to cultivate them.
5. Next, apply a thick layer of hay, pine needles, shredded leaves, sawdust, or bark-chip mulch over the newspapers. Water the strips to settle the newspapers and mulch. At this point, the garden should consist of mulched strips between cultivated rows.
6. Set out plants or seeds in the cultivated rows.
7. For subsequent plantings, turn under the mulched areas, which will then become the new planted rows. By the time the first crops have been harvested, the old mulch will be well on its way to decomposing and enriching the soil. In addition, this method results in crop rotation, which helps reduce disease and pest incidence.
8. For subsequent planting, mulch between the new rows (over the old ones) with the newspaper/mulch process.

Adhering to this method typically results in extreme ease of maintenance due to weed reduction. Another option for vegetable gardening is containers.

Container Vegetable Gardens

Colorful containers brimming with vegetables and herbs are one of the hottest gardening trends going today. Even harvesting is easier for vegetables that are container-grown or are in raised beds, since the crops will be somewhat elevated and therefore easier to reach and tend. Growing vegetables in containers filled with commercial potting mixes also ensures the absence of harmful nematodes and eliminates the possibility of soilborne insect and disease issues. Other benefits include the fact that potting soils are formulated to provide adequate drainage, moisture-holding capabilities, and often time-released nutrients. Specially designed container vegetables are just right for smaller spaces too. Here are some container vegetables suited for

'Trombocino' climbing squash maximizes available garden space.

Zones 8 through 11, with seasonal exceptions. Look for healthy seedlings in pots or six-packs or start plants from seed.

Cool-Weather Crops

Chard—try 'Bright Lights' and 'Pot of Gold.'

Lettuce and salad greens—try mesclun mixes and 'Pot and Patio Lettuce Blend-Varieties,' 'Garden Babies,' 'Ruby and Emerald Duet,' 'Miner's Lettuce,' 'Beetberry,' *Chenopodium capiatum*, arugula, *Shungiku* edible chrysanthemums, nasturtium, and viola.

Mustard—try 'Golden Streaks.'

Onion—try 'Tropeana Lunga,' an intermediate day red torpedo.

Radish—try 'Chinese Red Meat,' a large, sweet variety.

Spinach—try 'Regal' baby-leaf.

Warm-Weather Crops

Beans—try climbing varieties such as scarlet runner, 'Musica,' or 'Red Noodle.'
Cucumber—try 'Bush Slicer.'
Eggplant—try 'Twinkle.'
Pepper—try 'Chilly Chili,' 'Baby Belle,' and 'Pizza My Heart.'
Squash—try 'Trombocino,' a climbing summer squash.
Tomato—try determinate varieties, especially 'Super Bush.'

Routine garden maintenance starts with regular monitoring of what is going on. Deadheading annuals, pruning shrubs, picking produce as it matures, and providing the necessary moisture and nutrients are just some of what a successful gardener needs to do. Even when all of these chores are accomplished successfully, problems can and do arise. But early identification of the "big three" problems—weeds, insects, and disease—is a gardener's best defense. Left unchecked, these little problems can spell big trouble.

To Butterfly or Not . . .

Attracting butterflies brings color and movement to the garden, as well as plant-munching caterpillars.

∾ QUICK TIP

Container Tomato Success

Success with container-grown tomatoes relies primarily on the following:

- Rich soil, heavily mulched to suppress weeds and preserve moisture
- Consistent moisture; water faithfully every day
- Sunshine and temperatures 70°–80°F

2

Trouble in Your Paradise

Healthy, well-groomed plants located in the right places will be far less susceptible to the "big three" problems that typically affect Florida gardens:

1. Weeds
2. Insects and other pests
3. Plant diseases

Of course, having a few tricks up your sleeve won't hurt either. Low-care gardens can be just that, but they are not entirely without care. A bit of time spent avoiding these three issues to begin with can save time and trouble later on.

Pesticides and herbicides, organic or otherwise, are potent chemicals. Garden products with ingredients ending in "-cide" are meant to kill, and kill they do, often not discriminating between the good bugs and the bad, the good plants and the bad. The distinction between poison and medicine is directly related to dosage, so use pesticides and herbicides with caution and in direct compliance with all recommendations and directions. However, there are instances when the use of these chemicals is the only option left. In such cases it is wise to first contact your county Extension office for diagnosis, advice on whether or not to use chemicals, and, if needed, what chemicals are most effective.

Consumer demand and environmental regulations have prompted the development of safer pesticides and herbicides, and some of these new biochemicals use common ingredients such as corn or sugar to deter weeds and insects. Neem oil, insecticidal soaps, and BT (*Bacillus thuringiensis*) products are possible choices in this category. BT products are used to control caterpillars, leaf beetles, and mosquito larvae. The bacterium works by destroying the cell lining of the insect's gut, but note that only certain insects digest and are affected by the protein toxins. While these proteins have virtually no known effect won most insects (as well as people, birds, fish, and other animals), if butterflies are your passion BT is probably not your poison. Of course, the aforementioned injunction bears repeating: Use these powerful tools only as a last resort, and use them with due caution and according to directions. Wear protective clothing, gloves, and a respirator when handling all pesticides, herbicides, and fungicides.

Keeping plants healthy is the best defense against garden pests and diseases—this means checking them daily, handpicking insects, removing diseased plants before the trouble can spread, pulling weeds before they can take over, using compost, and watering appropriately. Do these things faithfully and chances are pretty good that you won't have to resort to the "cides."

Top Ten Ways to Deal with Weeds

It won't take long for weeds to discover the perfect little environment that you create in your gardens, be they inground or container plantings. Weeds are opportunistic and have evolved to take advantage of every growing situation and delivery method. When the tenacious air potato, *Dioscorea bulbifera*, showed up in my container plantings, it took a bit of detective work to discover that neighborhood squirrels had imported the noxious tubers and planted them in the pots. No garden is really safe from this sort of mischief, and with all weeds, if you give them an inch, they will take a mile.

While one person's weeds are another's wildflowers, you should show no mercy when it comes to evicting and preventing weeds. Weeds compete with other plants for water, nutrients, and sunshine. Prompt identification is vital. Familiarize yourself with the enemies, how they look at various stages from tiny seedling to full-blown flowering seed factories. Remove them before they go to seed and half the battle is won. Even if you do not catch them early, herbicides are doubtfully the answer, especially if your garden contains edible crops. Here are ten solid methods to rid the garden of weeds without a whiff of chemicals:

1. MULCH: Prevent weeds from gaining a foothold. A thick layer will discourage weeds from seeding, and a layer of landscape fabric underneath adds an even tighter barrier of protection.
2. PULL: Early hand removal of weeds will prevent their spread, and will also prove an easier task. *Never* allow weeds to go to seed, or the problem will be greatly multiplied. This is one of the best options.
3. SOLARIZATION: A layer of clear plastic is spread over the future garden area, sealed around the perimeter, and allowed to sit for at least a month. In addition to killing many weeds, this process can also knock back nematodes and soil pathogens.
4. HOE: Chop off weeds at ground level or just below with a scuffle or other hoe.
5. MOW: Closely crop with a power mower and repeat when necessary.
6. TURN: Use a shovel to turn weeds under, where they will decompose.
7. BOIL: Pour a thin stream of boiling water onto weeds.
8. CROWD OUT: Closely planted areas will prevent weeds from seeding in and shade out any that do manage to germinate.

9. BURN: Useful for really pernicious weeds, propane-fueled torches designed for weed removal can do the trick.
10. STOMP 'EM: When all else fails, this last resort is curiously gratifying, and will kill the weeds.

One more word of advice on weeds: Stop them before they grow with corn gluten. A flaky yellow product, corn gluten does not harm children, pets, or wildlife. It prevents seeds from germinating but has been found to be more effective at preventing weeds in lawns than in ornamental beds. Still, corn gluten can be applied several times a year and may stop a weed problem before it begins. As an added bonus, corn gluten eventually degrades, enhancing soil composition. Of course, use it according to directions.

The kettle method of weed extermination uses a stream of boiling water and is especially useful for removing weeds around paved areas.

Insect Pests

As easily as weeds can spoil your gardening fun, so too can insects, but while the first instinct may be to reach for the spray, remember that not all bugs are bad. Some of them, like ladybugs, praying mantises, walking sticks, parasitic wasps, dragonflies, as well as the pollinators (bees, bumblebees, and many wasps), are on your side. Pollinating insects such as honeybees are responsible for fertilizing not only ornamentals, but also most fruit and vegetable crops. In addition, some of the aforementioned insects help to eliminate many of those insect pests that attack your plants. Plus, there are microscopic parasites that are preying on those very pests eating your bush beans. When pesticides are employed, all of these friends of the gardener are often destroyed.

Furthermore, whether they are organic or not, all pesticides are inherently dangerous. If you simply must use one, carefully read its warning labels and follow the usage instructions—not only the health of your plants and their insect friends depend on it, but so does your own.

∾ QUICK TIP

Clean Fountains

Small recirculating fountains are a wonderful way to bring moving water into a garden. Because pets and wildlife often visit these fountains to drink, be sure to keep the water clean and slime-free. Do so by adding a tablespoon or two of cider vinegar to the water reservoir instead of bleach, which could harm any drinkers. The vinegar will also keep mechanical pump parts cleaner and free of mineral buildup.

We have already discussed the importance of growing healthy plants by providing them with the elements and environment needed to thrive. Healthy plants are better able to resist insect and disease damage. Keeping plants thriving is the best defense against problems, not pesticides.

∾ QUICK TIP

A Passion for Pollinators

Attract pollinators with specific plants. Bees, hummingbirds, butterflies, and some parasitic wasps can be tempted with plants such as firebush (*Hamelia patens*). Also, experiment to find out which plants are most attractive to pollinators and limit chemical use.

Remove insects early by hand to prevent plant damage.

- It only takes a minute or two each day to examine plants and detect any problems early on. This sometimes involves looking beneath as well as on top of plant leaves.
- If insects are present, first identify them as friends or foes. Pick harmful bugs from plants or knock them into a small jar of water mixed with dish detergent. Insect traps are dubiously beneficial—they often just attract insects.
- Those who grow butterfly gardens should expect caterpillars, because, after all, they are what produce butterflies. Because of this, host plants are grown to sacrifice to these hungry larvae. Often, the most vulnerable garden plants are those that produce vegetables and fruits. Keep this in mind should you decide to have both a butterfly garden and a vegetable plot.

∾ QUICK TIP

Who Knew . . .

You may know that hummingbirds are attracted to nectar and red flowers and are important pollinators, but did you realize that they also consume great numbers of insects? Just one more reason to plant red-flowering plants.

- Remember that birds and other wildlife are often allies in the battle against pests, so inviting them into the garden is to your advantage. Some birds can eat their own weight in insects each day! Bird feeders and pools of fresh water are two of the best ways to attract birds. Also, if there is room in your yard, a brush pile can offer a habitat for a variety of wildlife.
- Even snakes, such as the rat, rough green, and scarlet king snake, are valuable partners in this battle. Rough green snakes in particular are noted for helping eradicate the voracious lubber grasshoppers. Planting trees, vines, and shrubs, such as hollies or nectar-producing plants, will enrich the gardening experience, assist the gardener, beautify the surroundings, and invite natural allies.

Avoiding all the "cides"—pesticides, herbicides, and the like—will enrich your environment and make it safer for not just animals, but you, your family, and friends. If you must use chemicals, remember those safer choices: neem oil, BT (*Bacillus thuringiensis*) products, and insecticidal soaps. (See Plate 11.)

∿ QUICK TIP

Very Slinky

Keep squirrels off of the pole that supports a bird feeder with a springy wire toy. Place the Slinky® over the pole and attach the top of it to the bottom of the feeder. It will form a wobbly coil collar around the pole as it relaxes to the ground.

Other Pests: Keeping Four-Legged Creatures out of the Garden

There are some animals, cute though they may be, that are simply not welcome in the garden. One deer, for instance, can devour entire gardens in a single evening.

Squirrel Deterrent

A sprig or two of fresh rosemary tucked into pots will keep squirrels from digging in them, and will root more rosemary plants.

Called "200-pound rats" by some frustrated gardeners, deer often travel in herds, compounding the destruction.

Other animals such as skunks, squirrels, moles, opossums, and armadillos can literally plow up a flower bed in search of grubs, insects, or other food. In southern portions of the state, iguanas are becoming a real nuisance by eating fruit and even flowers and foliage. Some solutions for these pest problems include the following:

- Scent and taste: Commercial or homemade concoctions can be applied to plants to make them unappealing as food. Garlic, rotten eggs, and red pepper are some commonly used items. Occasionally, some of these mixtures can harm plants. In that case, try growing some plants that naturally repel pests. Try mothballs to keep squirrels or the neighbor's cat out of the garden.
- Water: Motion-activated devices direct a harmless blast of water at an animal intruder.
- Fencing: Lightweight, fibrous mesh fencing is easy to install and will keep most animals out. However, it needs to be tall enough to prevent deer from jumping over it—at least eight feet—and anchored to the ground to keep smaller animals from crawling or digging under it. A box-like cage can be constructed out of a rigid frame covered by mesh or chicken wire to protect choice plants or small beds.
- "Invisible" fence: Heavy-duty fishing line strung around a garden on posts at heights of one, two, and four feet will often prevent deer from entering by spooking them (since they can feel but not see it).
- Electric: Certainly the most hard-core fencing to exclude deer and other creatures. Install three levels of wire: the first at six inches, the next at two feet, and the third at four feet above the ground. Place tabs of aluminum foil smeared with peanut butter at various points around the fence to demonstrate to animals its shocking power. This way they will avoid it rather than try to jump over the fence.

∾ QUICK TIP

Blowin' in the Wind

Try employing one or even a squadron of festive pinwheels stuck in the ground or pots. These will rotate in the slightest breeze and the motion may scare critters away.

- Barrier: Keep dogs, cats, or other animals from digging in the garden with a layer of landscape fabric around plants. Cover fabric with mulch to disguise.
- Mole control: Moles dig tunnels, churning up ornamental or vegetable beds, even lawns, in search of grubs. They do not directly attack plants, but their tunnels can cause root damage. Treat planted areas for grubs at appropriate times of the year

with organic controls or simply leave them alone. Special mole-repellent sprays comprised of castor oil may also be effective. Again, you can also do nothing, because eventually the moles will move on when the grub supply is gone.

Plant Diseases: Identify and Act Early

Florida's hot and humid conditions can foster fungus and a host of diseases that can sicken and kill plants. Weather extremes such as cold or drought can weaken plants, allowing diseases to attack. The best defense against disease is to maintain healthy plants. Those species that are susceptible to fungus (roses, for instance) are best spaced widely to allow for good air circulation. However, disease sometimes strikes regardless of your efforts. Quick identification can often save the plant in trouble, and your county Extension office can often help you diagnose a plant disease problem and suggest a possible cure.

Frequently the best thing to do when a plant becomes diseased is to remove it *before* the infection spreads. Nursing a sick plant back to health, while gratifying, can sometimes mean infecting all the surrounding plants. To prevent this, you could isolate the plant in a separate pot for treatment.

When disease occurs in larger plants such as shrubs or trees, it is best to call experts who can determine whether the plant can be saved. It's certainly a tough choice, but such a sacrifice could stop the disease's spread. In any case, early detection and identification give the plant its best chance of survival.

Garden Smarter, Not Harder: Avoid Injury and Accomplish the Task Easily

Whether it's moving heavy containers or cultivating and planting, gardening is often strenuous. Gardening smarter means protecting oneself against a variety of injuries that can occur during both light and heavy tasks. Luckily, many new ergonomic gardening tools are designed to help ease the strain of repetitive movements such as pruning, raking, and lifting. But even the new, lightweight, non-ceramic planters can be heavy when filled with soil and plants.

Furthermore, your best gardening ally—Florida sunshine—can be an enemy to your skin. With skin cancer on the rise, protection is paramount. So, here is some sun sense for Florida gardeners:

- Wear a wide-brimmed hat and long-sleeved shirt for better sun protection.
- Before stepping out the door, prepare your hands for the work to come. A layer of sunblock (with a UVA/UVB Sun Protection Factor of at least thirty) is the first defense for your hands, and it should also be applied generously to your face, neck, and arms. For a gardener especially, ultraviolet rays can damage the tender

backs of the hands, eventually causing unsightly spots. Most creamy sunscreens also act as moisturizers, which does a little extra for your hands. In addition, look for a hand lotion with silicone for an added layer of protection in the garden.

QUICK TIP

Find 'em Every Time

Install a magnetic knife strip in the garage or anywhere garden hand tools are stored to keep them handy and organized.

Depending on what type of work is in the day's schedule—digging, weeding, raking, pruning, or setting out plants and seeds—it's usually a good idea to wear gloves. If your hands are going to be in the dirt, don a pair of heavy-duty kitchen gloves or neoprene gloves lined with knitted cotton fabric. Available gardening glove choices include those with plastic or neoprene-coated finger and palm areas for moisture protection and added grip. Such gloves help keep your hands dry and protected no matter the job. Cotton or supple leather gardening gloves are the better choice when digging or raking, as these help prevent blisters. Select gloves with gauntlet cuffs when working with roses or rough/thorny shrubbery.

QUICK TIP

Finger Tips

A nubbin of cotton from a cotton ball can be slipped into each of the tips of the finger holes in gardening gloves. This little cushion will help prevent soil from getting under your fingernails and protect the gloves too.

Even with such precautions, your hands will sometimes still get really grimy. That's when the fingernail brush and soap come out. There are some unpleasant things in our soil—fungus, for example—and it is because of this that it is important to wash away all traces of dirt from your hands and nails. A stiff fingernail brush is the best way to go, and although most soaps will kill germs, a few drops of hydrogen peroxide can be worked under your fingernails for extra protection from nail fungus. After all that scrubbing, your hands may be chapped and dry. A soothing herbal salve or a fragrance-free, oatmeal-based hand lotion can moisturize work-weary hands.

To protect your feet, wear closed-toe shoes or boots, not sandals. Feet also need protection from nail fungus, tetanus, and minor cuts and scrapes. Several styles of slip-on waterproof gardening shoes are now available, some with built-in foot and toe protection. When mowing, always wear closed-toe shoes or boots with good traction.

Even so, no matter how careful we are, cuts and scratches are ultimately inevitable. A good wash with soap, followed by germicidal spray or ointment and a sterile covering are what is called for in this case. Keep a selection of adhesive bandages on hand.

Also, make sure your tetanus booster is current. Tetanus, contrary to popular belief, does not require a cut by a rusty piece of metal to invade, but can be contracted through any break in the skin's surface, even a hangnail. Gardeners are prime targets of tetanus, and the disease is acute and often fatal. The characteristic symptoms are spasmodic muscle contractions and overall rigidity—a condition commonly known as lockjaw. Suffice it to say that tetanus prevention is not to be ignored.

Health officials now recommend a tetanus booster every ten years. The immunization is often administered in tandem with a diphtheria vaccine, as this is another infection which can be caused by a wound. The good news about tetanus is that the booster shot can be effectively administered up to seventy-eight hours after exposure. But it is best to plan ahead, and get the booster now.

❧ QUICK TIP

On the Other Hand

Whether you are right- or left-handed, you will probably get holes in and discard one or the other of your gardening gloves several times, thereby accumulating a supply of perfectly usable unmatched gloves. Just turn half of them inside out and use those new "pairs"!

Many of the tasks gardeners perform involve repetitive motions. Strong, repetitive gripping motions—think of using pruning shears, for example—can aggravate or create muscle and tendon damage in your hands and wrists. Risk factors for carpal tunnel syndrome—a painful and impairing condition—include vibration exposure, extreme postures, contact stresses, forceful exertions, and repetitive motion. Numbness and finger tingling are early symptoms of this problem.

❧ QUICK TIP

Easy Does It

Dedicate a pair of kitchen tongs to the garden to extend your reach when plucking weeds.

Fortunately, garden tool manufacturers are now creating hand tools with ergonomics in mind, and many modern tools reduce the risks involved. A few well-selected hand tools and accessories can help make gardening easier and avoid those scrapes, blisters, aches, and pains altogether. Indeed, a little caution and preparation will help ensure that gardening is as enjoyable as we expect it to be.

Gardening is full of physically demanding tasks—bags of soil and fertilizer, planters, and large pots often need to be moved. Avoid bending at the waist when working or lifting. Bend the knees, and when lifting, hold the object as close as possible to the body. Better yet, use an inexpensive hand truck or pot-lifting harness that can help move the heaviest items with ease. (See Plate 22.)

∾ QUICK TIP

Shop Vacuum Trick

Vacuum up, rather than rake, garden debris and leaves with a shop vacuum. Empty leaves onto the compost pile.

All the joys and benefits of a garden can be yours. With some planning, preparation, and care, the garden of your dreams can become a reality. All you really need is the desire and a speck of space and your garden can bloom gloriously. Some gardens, such as those described in the next chapter, can be realized sooner than you would think. Try starting one or more today.

3

Quick Garden Projects to Try Today

A Culinary Herb Box

Whether it be fresh chives to add to a baked potato or rosemary stems to use as herbal skewers in barbecue kabobs, fresh herbs are a cook's best friend. Furthermore, all culinary herbs aid digestion, so they are good and good for you.

Growing your own kitchen herbs means you don't have to remember to purchase parsley for that bowl of tabbouleh for the weekend potluck. It also ensures that you will have a ready supply of the freshest and tastiest herb varieties—sometimes even ones that may be hard to find locally. Maybe you can add fresh lemon basil to a pasta dish even though it has never before been available at your market. More and fresher varieties—that's what a kitchen-door herb box can deliver.

Planting an herb container garden.

Growing container herbs allows transport to sunnier locations with the change of seasons, which is important because most herbs require plenty of sunshine for best growth and flavor. Such mobility also enables you to whisk your box of tender herbs inside when low temperatures threaten.

Also, since some herbs (such as those in the mint family) tend to wander, growing them in a container will limit their unwanted spread. Keeping herbs trimmed and compact actually promotes fuller, bushier growth.

The garden described in this chapter focuses on culinary herbs, but there are many herbs for a variety of uses from culinary to medicinal to beauty products to tea, fragrance, and more. Visit a botanical garden or nursery that features herb gardens for inspiration or consult an herb book for ideas. Grow your favorite varieties or try something new to add an innovative dimension to your cooking. Whichever you pick, try to group your herbs according to their environmental requirements; for example, mints, parsley, dill, and chives prefer more moisture than do Mediterranean herbs such as rosemary, thyme, and oregano, which prefer somewhat drier soil conditions. A kitchen herb garden can be both attractive and fragrant, a little garden you will want to see and use daily.

You Will Need

- An appropriate container, preferably rectangular or square, approximately eighteen inches long by ten inches wide
- High-quality potting soil
- Your chosen herb plants

1. Fill the container about two-thirds of the way with a good commercial potting mix.

2. Choose four or five small, potted herbs. Select an assortment for a variety of uses, leaf forms, colors, and growth patterns (for instance, upright, bushy, and trailing). For this project, select only one plant of each variety desired. Here are some suggested species:

- Anise hyssop (*Hyssopus officinalis*); leafy upright growth, fragrant deep-blue flowers (height: 16–24")
- Basil; leafy upright growth (height: 16–18")
- Chives; spiky grass-like growth (height: 18")
- Cilantro; leafy (height: 12–18")
- Cuban oregano (see *Plectranthus*) (height: 18")
- Dill; delicate upright growth (height: 24"+)
- Lavender; lacy foliage, upright growth (height: 18–24")
- Lemon balm; leafy upright growth (height: 18–26")
- Lemongrass; tall, grassy growth (height: 18–48")
- Lemon verbena; leafy upright growth (height: 24"+)
- Mint; leafy, trailing growth (height: 18")
- Marjoram; trailing growth (height: 8–24")

- Oregano; trailing growth (height: 8–24")
- Parsley; leafy (height: 14–20")
- Rosemary; upright to bushy growth (height: 18–60")
- Sage; tall, leafy upright growth (height: 16–30")
- Thyme; trailing growth (height: 6–12")

3. Remove the selected plants from their pots, untangling the roots as possible to allow expansion, and then arrange them in the planter so that the tallest plants are centered and the next-tallest ones radiate toward the edges. Place herbs with trailing growth along the outside edges of the container. Add soil around the plants and water to settle it; place the container in a sunny location.

4. Allow the herb plants to at least double in size before beginning to snip and harvest them.

Instant Water Garden in a Pot

Gardeners everywhere are discovering the pleasures of water gardening, and it is one of the fastest-growing areas of interest. A water garden can be extremely satisfy-

Water gardens can go anywhere and create soothing accents.

ing and relaxing, with ever-changing patterns and plays of light on the surface of the water. Flowering water plants are available at most garden centers.

A simple water garden does not require weeding or fertilization. In fact, the only upkeep is topping off the water level. Because it is small and self-contained, it can go anywhere. If desired, live fish, such as mosquito fish (*Gambusia*) can be added to control mosquito larvae or other insects (see note on fish in materials list below). Snails can also be introduced to help clean the container.

You Will Need

- An attractive, glazed or unglazed terra-cotta pot or bowl with a two-gallon or greater capacity
- Cork or silicone sealant
- Clean gravel or coarse sand (play sand works)
- Aquatic plants
- Snails or fish if desired (fish have additional requirements like supplemental food, untreated water, biweekly partial water changes to reduce nitrate levels, and a small water or air pump for circulation/aeration)
- Fresh water

1. Select a container with a capacity of at least two to three gallons and plug the drainage hole with a snug fitting cork or sealant.

2. Place the container in a location that receives four to six hours of filtered sun per day. Elevating the water garden on a short base brings it closer to eye level. Also, it may be necessary to move the container to an area with more or less sun to enable healthy growth.

3. Place a small amount of rinsed sand or gravel in the bottom of the container. This will help anchor plants and provide a habitat for fish if they are added.

4. Fill the container with water. If you are using treated tap water and desire fish, either allow it to sit for two or more days or buy chemical dechlorination liquid at any pet or aquarium store.

5. Select two or three aquatic or semi-aquatic plants, preferably including one that floats on the surface (such as a lily), one that has upright growth (such as a miniature papyrus or arrowhead), and one that is entirely submerged.

6. Leave these plants in the containers in which they came. If using bare-root plants, first soak the potting medium (a mix of equal parts clean sand, gravel, and potting soil) and then place it around the roots in small terra-cotta or plastic pots. Arrange the potted plants in the water garden using rocks, bricks, or small terra-cotta pots so that they are at the appropriate level.

7. Add fish and snails, if desired (see their additional needs above, and as a general rule, only add about one one-inch fish per gallon of water capacity; additionally, monitor the water temperature for the first few days to make sure it is not too high—83°F or higher is too hot for most tropical fish).

8. Sit back and enjoy.

Container Culture for Color and Texture

When it comes to planting containers, think of the following three levels, which need to be considered for a well-balanced planting

1. High
2. Medium
3. Low or trailing

You Will Need

- An attractive pot
- High-quality potting soil
- A selection of bedding plants in six-packs or individual three- to six-inch pots

Varying plant forms, heights, and textures beautifies container gardens.

1. Fill your container two-thirds of the way with the commercial potting mix.

2. Select three different types of plants that provide those growth patterns, paying attention to bloom and foliage colors for good coordination. For instance, place bright-pink snapdragons (which have spiky upright growth) in the center. Then add something that grows to about half that height, say a pale-pink-flowered geranium, mounding petunia, or impatiens. The final choice should be something with a low growth habit, a plant that will spread over the edge of the pot to tumble down the sides of the pot, preferably adding color and texture—perhaps an ornamental sweet potato such as *Ipomoea batatas*, which, in its variegated form, displays chartreuse, pale pink, and white leaves. And although the ornamental sweet potato is a fast grower, if it is confined to a container it should be just fine. Most important, the sweet potato will continue to provide color when the other selections are not blooming, and its leaves add a nice textural component.

You may have noticed that this container suggestion is basically a monochromatic one in shades of pink. This is very chic, current, and easy to coordinate, since you only have to pick shades of one bloom color. Here is the combination:

- Deep-pink snapdragon
- Pale-pink geranium
- Variegated chartreuse/pink/white ornamental sweet potato

For a pot emphasizing texture in full sun, try combining the big, fleshy, red-tipped, and silvery leaves of a stunning kalanchoe (*Kalanchoe thyrsiflora*) with a tumble of 'Silver Falls' dichondra, which will create a silver cascade over the pot. Add a purple fountain grass like *Pennisetum rubrum* for a spectacular contrast and the result is a dramatic garden that simmers with texture and color to spare. Components:

- Kalanchoe (*Kalanchoe thyrsiflora*)
- 'Silver Falls' dichondra
- Purple fountain grass (*Pennisetum rubrum*)

3. Remove the plants from their containers and place plants with the tallest mature heights in the middle. Next, arrange the plants in descending order outward and put trailing or low-growth plants around the edges. Fill in everything with potting mix and water well.

Salad Bowl Garden

Few satisfactions rival picking a vine-ripened tomato or a basket of snap beans that you yourself grew. And certainly nothing tastes better or is better for you than those fresh-from-the-garden vegetables, especially when they are grown organically.

Thankfully, it doesn't take acres of land to achieve that goal. Even apartment dwellers can reap the benefits of a home garden. All that is needed is a sunny balcony or patio and a couple of containers to enjoy a bountiful harvest. New varieties

It will not take long for this garden project to produce fresh salad greens.

Three weeks later, and a crop of arugula and baby lettuce greens is nearly ready for harvest.

of vegetables suitable for container cultivation have helped hone such space-constrained gardens to perfection. Tender and crunchy little heads of lettuce such as 'Garden Babies' or mixed cutting greens are just right for containers. Compact tomato, eggplant, and pepper plants can be grown in just inches of space, and climbing varieties of beans, cucumbers, and squash help utilize every available centimeter of growing capacity as they climb. In short, practically anyone who wants to can grow their own vegetables.

This quick-growing project is best planted in fall or spring and will deliver weeks of the freshest salad greens. Don't be shy about adding edible flowers such as nasturtiums or marigolds or herbs to the containers for extra color, interest, and utility.

You Will Need

- A large terra-cotta saucer, eighteen inches wide by two inches deep, or a shallow bowl-like planter
- High-quality potting soil
- Mesclun lettuce, arugula, and radish seeds
- Trailing nasturtium seeds or basil seedlings if desired

1. Fill your container with the potting mix, preferably one that contains added nutrients, or add slow-release fertilizer granules to mix before planting seeds.

2. Place the container in a location that receives at least five hours of full sun daily, preferably with late-afternoon shade. It could also be placed in a small child's wagon or on casters for easier transport.

3. Plant the mesclun seeds in the center and radish seeds around the perimeter, according to seed package directions. If planting nasturtiums, select two to three spots near the edge of the planter and plant one or two seeds in each, or, if growing basil, place basil seedlings near the center.

4. Water the soil as needed. Terra-cotta containers dry out faster than do nonporous ones, but they do provide better drainage.

5. Inspect young plants for signs of insect damage and handpick any that are present. Move containers if more or less sun exposure is needed. In about three weeks you can begin harvesting the tender leaves of the mesclun and arugula for salads. Edible flowers will take a bit longer to mature.

Window Box Pizzazz

Old-world charm and new-world ease can be achieved with today's window boxes. Some planter box choices include built-in water reservoirs that reduce watering. Furthermore, painting and sanding are tasks of the past with new hi-tech window boxes. For the traditionalist, though, wooden or "hayrack" planters can naturally deliver just as much color and interest wherever they are used. Note that the latter will require more frequent watering, but the use of moisture-absorbing granules in the potting medium would help offset this.

Window box plantings, because of their locations, must include shorter plants that do not obstruct visibility. Select plants for color, texture, and low growth pattern. Consider colors that complement those of the intended building. Trailing plants, ivies and the like, are good choices for window box collections. But don't

Think outside the "box," adding vegetables or herbs such as this parsley to your own window box project.

A jumble of coconuts fills this window box during the hottest summer days, making the most of the unproductive weather.

rule out vegetables such as head and leaf lettuces, cherry tomatoes, colorful chard, herbs, or edible flowers such as nasturtiums, violas, and calendulas. These alternatives can bring color, texture, and a unique utility to window plantings.

Once mounted, window boxes can also be filled with items other than plants for inventive decoration during off-season or gardener absences. Consider, for instance, a window box piled full of green coconuts (leave the husk, or mesocarp, on) accented by a few choice seashells during the hottest summer months when most plants would wilt. Pinecones with a few evergreen boughs tucked here and there could stand in during winter. Possibilities are limited only by your imagination. But when it comes time to plant, the choices are truly grand.

You Will Need

- A window box planter and mounting hardware
- High-quality potting soil
- A selection of plants in six-packs or three- to five-inch pots

1. Install the window box first, thereby eliminating the obvious difficulty of trying to mount a filled box.

2. Fill the box two-thirds of the way with soil.

3. Select a variety of plants, bearing in mind the "rule of three"—high, low, and medium. Remove the plants from their containers, placing the tallest at the back, the medium ones next, and low-growing or trailing plants at the front. Group blooming plants in one to three bunches to increase color impact.

4. Fill in with soil and water thoroughly, continuing to do so as needed.

4

Gardening with Children

Starting children gardening early not only helps them achieve a sense of accomplishment, but it gives them an opportunity to assume some responsibility. Plus, it introduces youngsters to an activity that they may enjoy for the rest of their lives. If the gardening project focuses on a vegetable garden, it could even provide an incentive to get the little ones to eat their vegetables. There are plenty of ways to approach the concept.

Children take to gardening instantly and love to share their harvests.

A gardening project can occupy some of the boundless energy and curiosity of children, and it give them an experience that will teach them a thing or two about the way things grow. In a day and age when many children have minimal contact with nature, gardening can help reconnect them with the world in which they live, teaching them about soil science, insects, birds, other animals, and, of course, plants. A garden's lessons are those of wondrous nature.

You may learn a thing or two yourself as you observe how differently children experience gardening. When the children across my street saw me pruning some leggy plants, they asked for the clippings. As I continued trimming, they rushed back for more. I wondered what they were doing with all those clippings, and asked them if they were building a compost pile. They said they were playing "store," and the leaves and seeds represented "food" and "money." Children seem to have a natural affinity for plants. Indeed, there is such a thing as children's plant "lore," a tradition through which generations of children have handed down such "secret" things as the bit of sweetness that comes from sipping honeysuckle blossoms, creating "dancing ladies" from hollyhock blooms, or fashioning crowns and ringlets from flowers.

A Primrose Path

Make rustic garden paths sparkle with "magic." Use cast-off items—perhaps a chipped china cup, marbles, shells, coins, tiny toys, even old silver plate spoons. Treasures to discover at every turn.

Many towns now sponsor community gardens in which those lacking the room to garden can tend a small plot. Such projects allow everyone to experience the joys and rewards of gardening. The Junior Master Gardener program (www.jmgkids.us) is an excellent resource for children and adults alike, providing gardening projects, information, and supplies. Many local botanical gardens also sponsor children's gardens and programs.

A Garden of Their Own

If there is one mantra of children's gardening, it is this: Keep it simple! The idea is to help ensure success while providing something that will sustain interest.

Begin by giving the child their very own plot of earth or a large pot filled with a good soil, and have their space exist apart from your own. This will prevent the adult gardener from automatically assuming chores such as weeding, fertilizing, and watering out of habit. Let the child take responsibility and reap rewards on their own, as this can boost their sense of accomplishment. There will always be time later for them to perfect gardening techniques.

Help the child create a very small bed to start with, maybe a couple of feet square. A small raised bed created from scrap lumber, cement blocks, or bricks would be preferable and give the project some legitimacy. A small plot is important to keep the little agriculturalist from being overwhelmed by chores.

Assist the budding gardener by filling the raised bed with compost-enriched soil (they can help mix it if desired). A good soil base will help ensure their efforts are rewarded with a good crop of vegetables or flowers.

Next, take the child to the garden center and help pick out seeds or healthy seedlings. Bear in mind that larger seeds, such as those of nasturtiums, sunflowers, radishes, or squash, are easier to sow than those of, say, petunias or tomatoes. Whichever way you steer the child, remember to keep the selection simple and fast-growing. Early success will only increase their joy in this newfound activity. Here are some useful suggestions:

- One of the quickest vegetable crops to start from seed is the radish. Within only a few weeks young gardeners can harvest bright-red globes that only need a quick wash before eating.
- Bush beans are also easy to plant, and compact plants can produce big crops. They also can be eaten fresh from the bush, or you can help the child prepare fresh green beans in a healthy meal, as a side dish, or in a salad. Climbing beans, such as the scarlet runner, produce an edible crop as well as colorful red flowers that attract hummingbirds. Try the bright red flowers in salads. A pole "tepee" can be erected to allow these beans to climb, and, if large enough, can form a secluded play space for the young gardener.
- One cherry tomato seedling can ultimately produce basket after basket of kid-sized tomatoes.
- Sunflowers are a big favorite among young gardeners, and their sizable seeds are easily planted. They provide a crop that can be fed to birds come wintertime. Or save the seeds for next year's planting. A playhouse comprised of a small grove of tall sunflower plants can provide a refuge for youngsters. There are several miniature sunflowers that are just as much fun to grow, but you could also try mammoth 'Sunzilla' sunflowers that grow ten feet or taller.

- Buy a couple of marigold bedding plants to add instant color to the bed while other seeds are germinating. Show the child how to deadhead faded flowers and keep the plants blooming. Other children's favorites include 'Easter egg' radishes and tricolor pole beans that can be planted at the base of sunflowers, which they will climb up and around just as Jack's magical beans did. 'Raggedy Ann' zinnias are also a hit with the younger set.
- Nasturtiums' large seeds are easily planted and quickly grow mounds of colorful blossoms. Blossoms and leaves can be added to salads for extra color and a peppery accent. As an added benefit, nasturtiums will often reseed themselves. Educate the young gardener about which flowers and plants are edible, and which should be avoided.

A set of smaller, child-sized tools and a small watering can will help youngsters establish authority.

Of course you'll want to show novice gardeners how to look for insect pests and remove them before they get to be a big problem. This is one aspect of gardening that children will take to immediately, since most are innately fascinated by bugs. It would also be a good time to discuss beneficial insects and their role in pollination and natural pest management. Teach them to recognize the larval form of the ladybug, which looks like a tiny dragon. The role of earthworms, for example, is another excellent topic to explore. No doubt your own inner child will learn just as much from the experience as the child you mentor will. (See Plate 23.)

Quick-Growing Projects for Small Fry

There are a number of quick and easy gardening projects that can be accomplished with simple equipment and household ingredients. Here is a list of a few:

- Carrot tops can be sprouted into lush, fern-like dish gardens that last for weeks. Simply slice about a half-inch off the top of a carrot. Place this top in a shallow container, such as a Styrofoam produce tray. Make sure the tray is clean, then add about a quarter-inch of water to the bottom and place it on a sunny windowsill. Water it regularly to keep the tray from drying out, and routinely replace all remaining water with fresh. In a few days this carrot-top garden will sprout attractive, fern-like green foliage.
- Bird seed can also be used to plant a great children's garden. Any container with drainage will do, and should be filled with some good, rich soil. Next, have the child scatter seeds evenly over the surface, press them lightly into the soil, and water sparingly. Set the garden in a sunny spot, and in a few days the seeds will germinate, eventually developing into a variety of plants. Most are grasses, but the selection may include a sunflower, millet, or something else.
- Raid the dried bean selection for more seeds to plant—even popcorn will work!

The leafy top of a pineapple can be planted to grow a new plant.

- There are some larger seeds that you may not have considered planting—pineapples, for example. Help the little gardener slice the top portion off of a fresh pineapple, leaving about half an inch of pineapple flesh. Prepare a pot with soil and place the pineapple on top, pushing it slightly into the soil. Water as needed to keep the soil moist but not soggy and keep it in a sunny place. Eventually, this plant can be moved outdoors during warm weather, and may eventually form its own little pineapple.

∾ QUICK TIP

Pineapple Progress

Start that pineapple top out right. Trim it and tuck it into a cup or jar with a couple of inches of water, then leave it there for a few days until roots form, changing the water as needed. Once it develops a good root structure, plant it.

- Don't toss those sprouted potatoes. Instead, let the little ones plant them in rich soil outside for a potato patch. If they water, fertilize, and tend them carefully, the plants should bloom in a few weeks. Two or three weeks after flowering ends, the young gardeners can dig their own potatoes.
- A sweet potato can be sprouted in water to create an attractive plant. Look for ones that have not been treated to keep them from sprouting—an independent farm stand or farmers' market would be a good place to find such a potato. Then, choose a vase within which you can partially submerge the potato. Add water and place the tuber in a sunny spot. In a few days, the sweet potato will sprout lush foliage.
- Another big seed that can be sprouted is an avocado pit. With the pointed end up, insert three or four toothpicks around the center circumference of the seed and place it over a jar of fresh water, with the water level just touching the bottom of the seed. Place this jar in a sunny spot and watch as the roots and then the top sprout emerge. Once a good root system has formed, the little tree can be potted, but leave the top half of the seed out of the soil (don't worry, it will eventually deteriorate). Water as needed and give the little tree plenty of sun.
- Fairy houses—tiny rustic structures made of old bark, dry leaves, sticks, pine-cones, seeds, shells, pebbles, and so forth—don't actually grow anything, but are nevertheless fun. These wee "houses" are located in the garden or near a tree for any nearby fairies to move into. Fairies, as most children know, are tiny creatures that look after the life forces of living things and therefore are frequent magical garden visitors.

Chances are, no matter how you choose to do it, that when you give any child the gift of gardening, you introduce them to an activity that keeps on giving for the rest of their life.

5

Seasonal Garden Chores

Month by Month

January

For many parts of Florida, this month is one of the most active and productive in terms of gardening. To prepare a garden site for the coming growing season, turn and amend soil at least two weeks before planting.

Smooth and rake soil to remove weeds, leaves, and other matter. Florida vegetable gardens are usually prepared with mounded rows that allow for side irrigation when necessary that provide good drainage. Using a hoe, mound up the soil

Structure in the garden can take many forms. This handsome, carved coral fence is part of an old Key West garden.

in long, straight rows for planting, leaving enough room between rows for walking and working the plot. Place the hoe handle on top of the rows and gently press to create a straight depression for seeds. Repeat along the entire length of each row.

If desired, mulch the depressions between rows to help control weeds, conserve moisture, and moderate soil temperature. Layers of newspapers (printed with soy inks only) can be used for this purpose. If you do use newspapers, be sure to thoroughly wet or weigh them down to prevent them from being blown around.

Mesclun and cutting greens can be planted now, with additional plantings every two or three weeks to ensure continuous production. Plant such seed selections in a high-quality potting mix in flats or large, shallow bowl pots for easy access and quicker growth. Most greens will tolerate cold weather, but should be moved under cover if a hard freeze threatens. When the flats are finished producing, add their soil and any expended plants to your compost pile.

Lettuce, spinach, and cold-tolerant claytonia or miner's lettuce (an attractive and decorative plant in its own right) can be planted in flats or large terra-cotta saucers filled with a shallow layer of commercial seed-starting mix to be transplanted to the garden when seedlings are about three inches tall. Because lettuce seeds are so small, seedlings usually need to be thinned out when planted directly in the ground. This method actually speeds up production time so lettuce can be harvested sooner.

∾ QUICK TIP

Seeds of Wisdom

Small seeds, such as those of lettuce, herbs, and many annuals, can be mixed with coarse sand before sowing for even distribution.

January Vegetables to Start Indoors

Eggplant	Peppers (sweet and hot)
Herbs	Tomato

January Vegetables to Plant Outside

Beet	Green pea
Broccoli	Kale
Brussels sprout	Lettuce
Cabbage	Mesclun
Carrot	Onion
Cauliflower	Potato
Celery	Radish
Chard	Snow pea
Chinese cabbage	Spinach
Fava bean	Turnip

Harvest citrus varieties such as navels, blood oranges, honeybell tangelos, limes, lemons, kumquats, and grapefruit as needed. Many of these varieties will hold on the tree until temperatures warm up considerably later. Prune dead wood to shape trees before blooming begins in February.

꩜ QUICK TIP

The Bean That Likes It Cold

While most bush beans cannot tolerate cold weather, the fava bean thrives on it, so plant fava beans now. These attractive plants have bluish-green foliage and black-and-white-striped blooms.

In many areas of the state, hard freezes occur this month and often into late February, although some areas have witnessed temperatures below thirty-two degrees Fahrenheit as late as April. When freezes or frosts are predicted, many tropical and subtropical plants and trees will need cold protection, including most citrus varieties. In the case of citrus trees, it is especially important to protect the graft area so that even if the treetop is damaged, the graft will not be destroyed. If a freeze is predicted, thoroughly water plants one or two days before to provide additional cold tolerance. Here are five popular methods to protect tender plants, shrubs, and trees:

1. Cover plants, shrubs, or trees with frost blankets, sheets, or regular blankets. Anchor the covering material to the ground to seal in radiational heat emanating from the ground. Covers should be removed during the day to avoid overheating plants. Be aware that merely wrapping the top of the plant will not protect it.
2. Construct a fitted frame and cover it with clear plastic that does not touch the plant and can be removed or opened during the day to prevent overheating plants.
3. Pile tree trunks and shrub bases with soil to cover the graft area, but be sure to remove it as soon as possible to prevent insect or disease damage to trunks and limbs.
4. Wrap tree trunks and shrub bases with garden hoses through which water flows to help maintain a constant temperature. Avoid using a spray of water to protect plants. Water could freeze on branches, and the weight of the ice could cause them to break or it could damage plants.
5. Use a lightbulb as a heat source, but do not allow it to directly contact the plant (use outdoor-rated fixtures and do not chain extension cords, if used).

Pruning and trimming shrubs, hedges, trees and perennials can be done late in this month, but wait to prune freeze-damaged plants until new growth emerges to avoid cutting away too much of the plant. Hydrangeas and azaleas will have already formed buds for spring flowers and should therefore not be pruned at this time. Here are some more pruning pointers:

Think Small

Rather than spend your time pruning crape myrtles, select new dwarf varieties that stay compact yet provide plenty of blooms. Many of these new varieties are also resistant to mildew problems.

- Prune the tops of peach and nectarine trees when planting this month. Remove up to a third of these trees each January, creating a bowl-like shape of the remainder of the tree to promote strong limbs and good fruit production.
- Sapodilla, guava, mango, and sugar apple trees can be pruned similarly.
- Ornamental grasses can be pruned now, and dead portions should be removed. Trim remaining portions of grass clumps, cutting away long shoots to create a well-formed clump.

Hold off on fertilizing until later in February or early in March as many plants are dormant now. Continue a regular watering schedule for roses, ornamentals, fruits, and vegetables because this month can often be dry. However, some plants, such as clivias and dormant bulbs, should be watered sparingly as they too are dormant now. For clivias, wait until buds form in spring to resume regular watering and fertilizing.

January is also a good time to replace mulch and, if necessary, landscape fabric. Cool temperatures and lack of insects make this one of the best months of the year to establish new ornamental beds or rework old ones. Many hardy perennials, shrubs, and vines can be planted now. Wait until the danger of freeze and frost is over (usually around late February to March, depending on your area) before setting out tender or tropical perennials and annuals.

Sweet peas (which, despite their name, are inedible), snow peas, and green or "English" peas (the latter two of which are edible) can be sown now as well. Provide supports for peas at the time of planting to avoid disturbing tender roots once plants begin to grow.

Plant cool-weather annuals including pansies, carnations, poppies, snapdragons, and violas, but be prepared to provide freeze protection to petunias, geraniums, and other tender annuals, herbs, and perennials as well as citrus and other tropical plants when freezes threaten.

QUICK TIP

Clean and Fragrant Bathwater

To help keep birdbath water fresh and discourage slime development, add a sprig or two of fresh lavender or rosemary to the water when refilling.

Keep bird feeders filled for winter visitors and year-round avian residents, and have fresh water handy for birds. For hummingbirds and other birds that do not visit the birdbath, install a bird mister, which can be found at wild bird supply stores. Instead of using hummingbird feeders, plant red-flowered annuals, perennials, and vines with tubular blossoms which will attract and feed hummingbirds. In addition to sipping nectar, hummingbirds are voracious insect eaters.

Some Nonaggressive Plants to Attract Hummingbirds

Cat's whiskers (*Orthosiphon stamineus*)
Cigar flower (*Cuphea ignea*)
Cleome (*Cleome* spp.)
Flowering maple (*Abutilon hybridum*)
Gingers (*Hedychium* and *Costus* spp.)
Hibiscus (*Hibiscus* spp.)
Horsemint (*Monarda punctata*)
Lophospermum (*Lophospermum erubescens*)
Pentas (*Pentas lanceolata*)
Salvia (*Salvia* spp.)
Shrimp plant (*Justicia brandegeana*)

February

In some areas, lawn mowing will be necessary in the winter months, but not as frequently as in summer. Use this downtime to do routine lawn mower maintenance: change the oil, lubricate the bearings, and, most important, sharpen the blade. Set mower height to cut to three inches. As previously mentioned, when cropped too short, grass develops shallow, unhealthy root systems that are not drought resistant and which will be more susceptible to weed problems.

Mow Saint Augustine grass to three inches, centipede to one and a half inches, and Bahia grass to three to four inches tall. Uneven lawn areas can be leveled by applying sand, but use thicknesses of no more than one inch to avoid grass damage.

Removing grass clippings is counterproductive. Clippings do not create thatch buildup and can provide natural nutrients as they break down over time.

Many trees, including live oaks, are now dropping leaves. Keep leaves raked from lawns, shred them, and add to compost or use as a mulch in ornamental and vegetable beds.

Clean, oil, and sharpen garden tools so they will be ready to work through the growing season.

Got extra seeds left over? Don't trash them, stash them in a heavy plastic baggie or container that can be tightly sealed, then store in the freezer until ready to use. Seeds stored in this manner should be good for at least a year or two.

Cold-weather vegetables, including carrots, can still be planted at this point. This is also a good time to plant lettuce, spinach, and arugula in the garden. Late in the month, bush beans, pole beans, and summer squashes can be planted in most areas, but freezing weather or a late frost will kill these tender plants. Still, it is probably worth the risk to get a head start on these crops now, being prepared to replant later if necessary. It is also safe to plant potatoes in most regions.

If big, sweet onions are your goal, plant onion plants, not the bulb-like onion sets or seeds. Florida gardeners will achieve the best results with plants. To plant, dig a trench about four inches deep and lay down a line of time-release fertilizer beads, then cover with a shallow layer of soil before putting in the little plants. Water regularly.

QUICK TIP

Invitation for Butterflies

Provide host plants to feed developing butterflies. Host plants include parsley, fennel, milkweed, citrus, and passion vines (*Passiflora* spp.).

February Vegetables to Plant

Beets	Kale
Broccoli	Lettuce
Brussels sprout	Mesclun
Cabbage	Onion
Carrot	Pea
Cauliflower	Potato
Celery	Radish
Chard	Snow pea
Chinese cabbage	Spinach
Fava bean	Turnip
Green pea	

Dormant grapes can be pruned now. Muscadine and scuppernong grapes are well-suited to Florida and produce fruit in late summer. Do any transplanting early this month to allow the plants time to establish.

Plants which were damaged by cold can be safely pruned provided that new growth has started. Pruning prior to this could result in too much being cut away and that could stress the plant.

Prune many shrubs (except for azalea and hydrangea), fruit trees such as apples, peaches, and pears, other dormant shade and fruit trees, as well as hybrid tea roses now through the end of this month.

For hybrid tea roses, remove all foliage from the plant and cut it back by about a third. Sculpt the plant into a vase-like shape by removing all ingrowing stems. For heirloom or bush roses, cut back and shape bushes as needed, removing any dead or diseased wood, which should be discarded.

Begin a neem oil spray regimen to help prevent aphid damage (effectiveness against black spot is questionable). Always water roses and other fungus-susceptible plants early in the day so that foliage can dry before sunset. Or, better yet, use soaker hoses that direct water to the roots, rather than on the foliage.

Bare-root and potted trees and plants can now be planted. This is also the time to transplant trees, shrubs, and perennials. Water any transplants well and apply water-soluble fertilizer, fish emulsion, and/or a root-stimulating concentrate to help plants quickly establish. Keep soil around plants moist but not soaking wet.

Harvest grapefruit, tangelos, tangerines, lemons, limes, and juice oranges as needed. In most areas, citrus trees will begin blooming by Valentine's Day. If a wide variety of citrus trees is planted, harvests can be extended for up to seven months as selections ripen, beginning with satsumas, which are often ready to pick in late October, and going through Valencia oranges, which ripen last and extend the harvest through the late spring. Many limes and lemons produce varying amounts of fruit throughout the year, blooming sporadically much of the year. (See Plate 9.)

∾ QUICK TIP

Invitation for Bees

A number of native and nonnative plants provide bee-attracting pollen, including, but not limited to:

- Cabbage palm (*sabal palmetto*)
- Gallberry (*Ilex glabra*)
- Saw palmetto (*Serenoa repens*)
- American holly (*Ilex opaca*)
- Ligustrum (*Ligustrum* spp.)
- Wild coffee (*Psychotria nervosa*)
- Citruses (*Citrus* spp.)

If there are several citrus trees in your yard and neighboring properties, and you are sure that no family members or friends have a serious bee allergy, consider inviting a beekeeper to place a hive in your yard. Your trees will benefit from more pollinators and the bees will have a good food supply.

Though many commercial beekeepers hire their hives out to large-scale growers throughout the state and beyond, many hobbyists keep bees in Florida and would probably not charge a fee. To locate a local beekeeper, contact your county Extension office or visit the Florida State Association of Beekeepers' Web site at: www.floridabeekeepers.org.

Honeybees (which are not native to North America) are generally on the decline, so native pollinators (some four thousand species in all!) become more valuable every day. This population shrinkage alone is a good reason to reconsider pesticide use, since many indiscriminately kill all insects. In addition to native pollinating bees and wasps, some moths and birds also pollinate.

Azaleas begin blooming early and should not be pruned until after their bloom period ends in late spring. Also, apply an acid fertilizer after blooming ends according to directions. Fertilize sparingly to avoid burning plants and watch for iron deficiency, typified by leaves turning pale and exhibiting yellow veins. Finally, maintain a regular watering schedule throughout these dry months.

Azaleas can be transplanted after blooming, but be sure to keep them watered until established.

A honeybee hive in the garden or home fruit tree grove will enhance pollination, so invite a local beekeeper and you will both benefit.

Visit the numerous garden shows and events throughout the state now and in the coming months for inspiration, plants, and supplies.

Also try a plant exchange. Divide perennials, make root cuttings, or plant extra annual and vegetable seedlings to share. Invite other gardeners well in advance so that they too can prepare for the exchange. Set a date a month ahead (to allow plants to establish) and ask each participant to bring at least ten well-established plants that are potted and labeled for identification and care.

At the event, have each person describe their offerings—the growing conditions required, mature size, bloom color and timing, and so forth. After everyone has done so, allow each person to select their first plant, repeating the rounds until everyone has ten plants. This ensures everyone goes home with new plants and an earful of gardening wisdom and information—all for free.

February Annuals to Plant Outside

Anise hyssop
Annual phlox
Bells of Ireland
Calendula
Caladium
Carnation
Cleome
Dianthus
Larkspur
Lisianthus
Lobelia

Marigold
Melampodium
Nasturtium
Nicotiana
Ornamental cabbage and kale
Pentas
Petunia
Poppy
Snapdragon
Stock
Zinnia

Lemongrass, popular in Thai cooking, grows tall and is an attractive plant in the landscape.

Many flowers can be used to make unique herbal teas or to add to salads. As blooms mature, harvest calendula petals or whole flowers and anise hyssop blossoms and dry them for tea mixes.

Collect the fresh blossoms of pansies, violas, or nasturtiums to use in salads to add a peppery nip and some color. Allow nasturtiums to go to seed and then collect the green seeds to pickle as imitation capers or let them reseed for another year of blooms.

Gather the first wild violet blossoms to add to spring salads for good luck and a dose of vitamin C.

Growing and gathering your own food can be fun and healthy. However, always exercise caution and be able to positively identify anything you plan to eat. Some, such as the colorful and prevalent yellow jasmine, can be deadly. Consult a good guide, such as the Peterson Field Series *Eastern/Central Medicinal Plants* by Steven Foster and James A. Duke, to identify any wild or unfamiliar cultivated plant, flower, or herb intended for the dinner table.

March

This is another busy month in the garden with many plants, shrubs, and trees flowering or leafing out. Fertilizer can be applied in early March to most trees, roses, and other shrubs and plants. Examine citrus leaves for the yellowish veins and pale coloration indicative of iron deficiency. If this problem is observed, supplemental iron may need to be applied in addition to a citrus-formula 6-6-6 or 8-8-8 fertilizer. Apply according to package directions or at a rate of one to two pounds of fertilizer per inch of trunk measured four feet from the ground and water in well.

∾ QUICK TIP

Power Watering

Make the most of this precious resource; when you water, try:

1. Timers to water during appropriate hours
2. Soaker hoses to deliver water where needed
3. Drip irrigation for perfect, efficient watering

There are many fertilizers on the market, including slow-release beads, water-soluble crystals, and liquids such as fish emulsions, plus bulk bagged varieties that come in five-, ten-, forty-, and fifty-pound bags for broadcast spreading.

As with most things, when it comes to fertilizers, you get what you pay for. Oftentimes organic and slow-release varieties are the costliest, yet they are usually the best choices as they release their nutrients slowly and over a period of time. Some contain nutrients that are more easily absorbed by plants, and their higher price reflects this benefit. The numbers on a bag of fertilizer, as in 8-8-8 or 16-4-8, represent the ratios of nutrient concentration:

1. The first number indicates nitrogen
2. The second number is phosphorus
3. The third number is potassium

Essentially, this means that in an 8-8-8 fertilizer, for instance, you have equal parts of all three nutrients, whereas in a 16-4-8 fertilizer, you have twice as much nitrogen as potassium, and four times as much nitrogen as phosphorus. This is important because different plants require different nutrient ratios.

Many fertilizers, such as those formulated for citrus, pecan, palm, or avocado, also have trace nutrients like calcium, magnesium, copper, and so forth. These are usually listed on the guaranteed analysis.

Begin harvesting Valencia oranges as they ripen, and continue to pick honeybell tangelos, blood oranges, and the remaining citrus varieties as needed. Orchard orioles, catbirds, woodpeckers, and other birds will enjoy overripe fruits and the insects they attract if left on trees.

It's time for baby birds—be on the lookout for nests in trees and shrubs and postpone pruning jobs around where they are located.

Put in more lettuce and spinach seeds or seedlings to get going before temperatures rise. Plant tomato seedlings deep to promote more roots along the stems.

❧ QUICK TIP

Best-Dressed Tomatoes

When planting tomato seedlings in the garden, insert a partially buried collar made out of an empty cardboard tube or a plastic cottage cheese container (with the bottom removed) into the soil around the plant to discourage cutworms. These collars also provide a convenient watering well.

During March, harvest *Brassicaceae* family vegetables, such as broccoli, Brussels sprouts, cabbage, kale, Chinese cabbage, cauliflower, and snow peas and radishes.

Keeping beans and peas picked as they mature can also help extend harvests as it prompts plants to produce more. Inspect plants regularly to head off any insect invasions, squashing any (garden gloves for the squeamish) you do find. Or, handpick and drop them in a small jar of soapy water.

Plant seedlings of parsley, chives, dill, oregano, marjoram, thyme, and basil in a large pot or planter to keep by the kitchen door for quick, easy access. Add some extra dill in the butterfly bed for feeding monarch butterfly larvae. Also, try several different varieties of basil, from the spicy deep-purple selections to fragrant lemon basil.

March Vegetables to Plant

Bush bean	Pepper, sweet and hot
Cantaloupe	Pole bean
Chard	Spinach
Corn	Summer squash
Cucumber	Tomato
Eggplant	Watermelon
Lettuce	Zucchini
Mesclun	

Start ornamental gourds in small pots indoors to plant outside when it is warmer. Prepare a sunny bed with rich soil. Provide them with plenty of moisture and nutrients throughout the growing period, as well as sturdy supports once outdoors. Many gourd vines will climb ten feet or higher, and some gourds can weigh several pounds, depending on the variety.

✎ QUICK TIP

A Native Pumpkin

Florida gardeners looking for a suitable pumpkin variety should try the Seminole pumpkin (*Cucurbita moschata*), also known as the wild squash of the Everglades. Resistant to insects and disease, these productive vines produce three-pound pumpkins that are just right for pies or other projects.

Allow gourds to dry on the vine before harvesting them for craft projects. Gourds will mature in the fall. When gourds are completely dry and the seeds rattle inside, they can be used in various craft projects or to create purple martin nesting houses. For more information on growing and using gourds, visit the Florida Gourd Society's Web site at www.flgourdsoc.org.

Caladiums can be started now. Removing the central bud from the tuber when planting encourages more leaf production.

Amaryllis comes into bloom. Be on the lookout for packs of immature lubber grasshoppers, which are one-inch, yellow-striped black grasshoppers that love to eat amaryllis. Instead of using pesticides to eradicate them, handpick or step on them.

✎ QUICK TIP

The Grasshopper Dance

Everybody quick now! Hop to it and stomp those little lubbers.
Do-si-do and clomp your feet. Don't you blubber!
There's no spraying to it. Ah, that's so sweet.

Loropetalum blooms in March with masses of pink blossoms, and camellias are ending their bloom period. In many areas, bougainvilleas are in bloom. (See Plate 13.)

Watch for snakes now and welcome them into your gardens. The majority of Florida snakes are nonpoisonous, and they aid the gardener by eating insect and rodent pests. March and October are active months for snakes. In March they move out of their winter resting places and head for summer hunting grounds.

In October they migrate to higher, drier locations to hibernate for the winter. Rough green snakes especially relish lubber grasshoppers, but Eastern black racers, rat snakes, and others are your garden allies as well. Sometimes the only evidence of their presence is a telltale snakeskin. Refer to a reptile field guide to accurately identify these slitherin' visitors for personal safety, but let them go on their way without harming them.

March Annuals to Plant for Seasonal Color

Anise hyssop	Marigold
Annual phlox	Melampodium
Bells of Ireland	Nasturtium
Calendula	Nicotiana
Caladium	Pentas
Cleome	Petunia
Dianthus	Snapdragon
Gladiolus corms	Stock
Jewels of Opar	Sweet Annie
Larkspur	Zinnia
Lobelia	

Butterfly amaryllis, 'Papilio,' is usually one of the first of these beautiful bulb flowers to bloom in early spring.

Be sure to water regularly during this traditionally dry month and deadhead annuals daily to promote continuous blooms. Apply water-soluble fertilizer to annuals and vegetables to promote growth.

April

Temperatures begin to climb, and little rain falls this month. Many crops, such as beans, onions, lettuce, spinach, and tender squash, should be at or near harvest time. Some early tomatoes will already have ripening fruit. Keep suckers (small lateral shoots sprouting from the lower part of the plant) removed from the main stems and the plants supported. If allowed to touch the ground, tomatoes may suffer insect damage or rot. Water tomatoes daily to ensure a good harvest, and reduce fertilizer application once plants set fruit.

❧ QUICK TIP

Color Them Naturally

Use natural dyes from foods such as purple grapes (purple-blue), onion skins (yellow-orange), blueberries (blue), beets (red), or spinach leaves (yellow-green) to color Easter eggs.

Use bricks or disposable aluminum pie pans beneath cantaloupes to keep the fruit off the ground as it matures; this will help prevent rot and insect damage. Also, plant heat-tolerant varieties of spinach and lettuce for one last crop before real hot weather sets in.

April Vegetables to Plant for Hot-Weather Harvest

Asparagus bean	Okra
Bush bean	Pepper, sweet and hot
Cantaloupe	Pole bean, especially Asian "noodle" varieties
Chayote squash	Summer squash
Corn	Sweet potato
Cucumber	Watermelon
Eggplant	Zucchini
Lima bean	

Cannas, Louisiana iris, and many of the terrestrial orchids such as nun's orchid (*Phaius tankervilliae*) bloom now, as do many crinums. Daylilies (*Hemerocallis* spp.) begin to set buds or scapes once nighttime temperatures are consistently sixty degrees Fahrenheit or higher. Additionally, daylily buds are edible and can be lightly steamed and served as a colorful side dish.

Clivia (*Clivia miniata*) blooms in late spring, so reduce water during winter and provide cold protection until this flowering plant comes out of dormancy.

Clivias should be in bud or flower now, and a regular regimen of water and fertilization can be resumed. Water rex, tropical angel wings, and hard cane begonias only sparingly after their soil has completely dried.

In April, gardenias come into bloom in northern portions of the state, and bougainvillea should still be in flower.

Continue to replace cool-weather annuals with heat-loving ones in planters and beds for constant seasonal color.

April Annual Varieties to Plant

Alyssum
Anise hyssop
Caladium
Celosia
Cleome
Coleus
Dusty miller
Gazania
Gladiolus
Impatiens
Marigold
Melampodium
Ornamental pepper

Pentas
Periwinkle
Portulaca
Salvia
Statice
Strawflower
Sunflower
Sweet Annie
Torenia
Verbena
Wax begonia
Zinnia, try fungus-resistant varieties

Orchids and other tender houseplants kept indoors through the winter can now be placed outside in appropriate light conditions. Many orchids will benefit from the increased humidity levels found outdoors, but will still need supplemental moisture until the rainy season begins later in the summer.

Harvest lavender blooms when buds are still tight by cutting the long stems and bundling them with a rubber band. Hang bundles upside down to dry out of the sun to use in dried arrangements or for potpourri. Or use the buds in herbal tea.

Lavender blooms can be dried for use in everlasting arrangements, potpourri, baking, or herbal teas.

∾ QUICK TIP

The "Sauce" for Butterflies

Nectar plants that attract butterflies include:

- Black-eyed Susan (*Rudbeckia hirta*)
- Butterfly bush (*Buddleia officinalis*)
- Lantana (*Lantana camera*)
- Milkweed (*Asclepias* spp.)
- Pentas (*Pentas lanceolata*)
- Phlox (*Phlox paniculata*)
- Porterweed (*Stachytarpheta* spp.)
- Scarlet sage (*Salvia coccinea*)
- Verbena (*Verbena spp.)*

Many trees, such as this *Magnolia grandiflora*, offer blooms that add to a garden setting.

Prune rosemary shrubs and plants to maintain a desired shape and use the clippings fresh as seasoning or dry to use later. Rosemary sprigs can be used as disposable sauce brushes for barbecue sauce. Or, strip leaves from sturdy, woody stems and use stems while still green as skewers for savory barbecue.

🌱 QUICK TIP

Earth Day

April is a time to celebrate our bountiful and beautiful Earth by going organic in the garden.

Plan an Easter or spring banquet or a tea with a floral theme out in the garden, thereby beating the heat and bugs that are sure to come soon.

May

Remember that old May Day tradition? Pick a little nosegay of fresh flowers, tuck them into a handmade paper cone that you've decorated with paper doilies, ribbons, or lace, then hang it on your neighbor's doorknob, ring the doorbell, and *run!* It is an excellent way to share a bounty of May flowers.

Harvest Valencia oranges, limes, and lemons as they ripen. Snap suckers off of citrus and other fruit trees like peaches, pears, and mangoes.

Speaking of fruits, peaches, plums, and nectarines also ripen this month; harvest them accordingly.

∾ QUICK TIP

Try Chayote

Try something new—chayote, from south of the border, is a squash-like vegetable that can take Florida heat. Its climbing vines grow all summer and then produce heavy crops of fist-sized squash in the fall.

Blackberries, both wild ones and cultivated varieties such as 'Brazo,' 'Flordag-rand,' and 'Oklawaha,' ripen now. After the berries are harvested, plants should be cut back to the ground. Apply a thick layer of mulch to discourage weeds.

∾ QUICK TIP

Spread the Harvest

Berries are easy to freeze. Place clean, dry berries in a single layer on a cookie sheet and freeze. Once frozen, seal them in plastic freezer containers or bags. Use frozen berries in muffins, quick breads, pancake batters, or simply as a frozen treat. They can also be thawed to make jams and jellies. Freezing is an especially good way to accumulate enough berries for a batch of jam if harvests are skimpy or drawn out over a period of time.

Hybrid tea and heirloom roses should be gloriously blooming now, including the thorny but endearing seven-sisters climbing roses. Continue a regular spraying regime with neem oil (according to package directions) to combat aphids. Fertilize roses with a slow-release rose fertilizer and water it in well. Roses need at least an inch or two of rainfall per week—more as temperatures climb. Irrigate if necessary to supply enough moisture. (See Plate 2.)

Clematis vines bloom now. Remember to provide enough moisture to these perennial flowering vines throughout the year so that they do not dry out, but are not left soggy.

Many perennials can be divided now for extra plants or to share with other gardeners. Use a liquid root-stimulating hormone mixed according to directions before and after dividing any plants.

May Heat-Loving Annuals to Plant

Alyssum
Anise hyssop
Caladium
Celosia
Cleome
Coleus
Dusty miller
Gazania
Gladiolus
Impatiens
Marigold
Melampodium
Ornamental pepper

Pentas
Periwinkle
Portulaca
Salvia
Statice
Strawflower
Sunflower
Sweet Annie
Torenia
Verbena
Wax begonia
Zinnia, try fungus-resistant varieties

June

Temperatures really begin to increase this month, although summer rains often have yet to appear. Continue to provide supplemental water to vegetables, ornamentals, and fruit and nut trees.

Tomatoes should be at their prime now. Extras can be frozen for use later, but nothing beats the taste of a freshly picked, vine-ripened tomato. Try them with a sprinkle of freshly chopped lemon basil, a drizzle of good extra-virgin olive oil, and a splash of aged balsamic vinegar. Or, combine that with a slice of homemade bread and some fresh mozzarella, and you have a meal.

❧ QUICK TIP

Top Ten Heirloom Tomatoes

Brandywine (pink)
'Cherokee Purple' (purple/black)
'Paul Robeson' (purple/black)
'Aussie' (red)
'Julia Child' (pink)
'Black Cherry' (purple/black)
'Kellogg's Breakfast' (orange)
'Gold Medal' (yellow-and-red-striped)
'Aunt Ginny's Purple' (purple/black)
'Carmello' (red)

To improve or change the fruit of an established citrus tree, try budding. Summer is the best time to bud or graft in new wood. Consult a fruit culture manual or contact your local county Extension office for more information.

Blueberries ripen this month. Pick daily.

Summer rains should begin late this month in many areas, making it a good time to fertilize fruit trees by applying appropriately around the trees' drip lines (the area marking the outer edge of the canopy). Many fruit trees have shallow feeder roots that extend out three times the diameter of their drip lines. Always remember to water in fertilizers well.

For citrus trees, it is advisable to keep the area from the drip line to the tree trunk free of weeds and grass. This prevents the grass or other plants from competing for nutrients and moisture and thereby allows for more efficient fertilization and irrigation.

Sunflower heads can be harvested and dried to use to feed birds and other wildlife.

Many annuals can also be dried to use in arrangements and craft projects. Dried flowers, also called everlastings, are simply flowers that have been hung to dry. Dried flowers can be used for long-lasting floral arrangements or worked into any number of craft projects—wreaths, framed arrangements, holiday decorations, and more.

Knowing which flowers dry best and which flowers retain their colors is the key to success with everlastings. Flowers that have thin, rather than thick or succulent petals are the best choice. Harvest blooms early in the day as soon as dew has dried and as the flowers begin to open. Gather several stems of like-colored flowers and bind them with a rubber band. Drying and storing like colors together makes using them easier than separating colors once they are dried.

Dry flowers by hanging them upside down in bunches in a warm and dry location out of direct sunlight.

Hang these bunches upside down in a warm, dry location out of direct sunlight, which will fade blooms. An attic or garage makes an excellent drying location. Here are some flower and foliage choices to grow that hold their colors and shapes well when dried:

Amaranth: 'Love Lies Bleeding,' 'Hot Biscuits'
Anise hyssop
Artemesia: 'Sweet Annie' (very fragrant)
Baby's breath
Bells of Ireland
Celosia: Cock's comb; Wheat celosia (pink)
Gomphera
Horsemint (*Monarda punctata*)
Lavender
Larkspur
Ornamental grass: 'Lime Light' millet, 'Purple Majesty,' Sorghum 'Bicolor'
Poppy seed heads
Salvia: Cambridge series
Statice
Stock
Strawflower
Yarrow
Zinnia

ᕽ QUICK TIP

Myrtle Incentive

To promote another crape myrtle bloom, remove seed heads and dead flowers.

Compost spent vegetable plants and annuals. Turn pile to aerate. No compost pile?

This is a good time to establish one to use vegetable, fruit, and yard trimmings to make soil amendments for free. Any spot will do, although you might want to screen the pile from view. Compost "works" quickly in the Florida climate, and no special equipment is needed (although there are many commercial composting tools on the market).

However, Florida's high temperatures and intense sunshine will actually burn up compost only one summer after it is added to beds. Mulching will slow this process, but even so, compost should be reapplied and thoroughly worked into beds often for lasting effect. In short—keep the compost coming.

A plastic milk crate makes a handy compost sifter.

June Annuals to Plant

Caladium
Celosia
Coleus
Dusty miller
Gazania
Impatiens
Melampodium
Ornamental pepper

Pentas
Periwinkle
Portulaca
Salvia
Sunflower
Torenia
Wax begonia

July

The dog days of summer begin in this month because Sirius, the Dog Star, becomes visible in the Northern Hemisphere's night sky. Summer heat and humidity can promote insect and fungus damage to lawns, so watch for chinch bug damage if you have Saint Augustine grass, and, if necessary, treat with an approved insecticide. Areas damaged by chinch bugs do not recover, so treat the area, remove dead grass, and replace it with new sod or plugs. Also, watch for mole cricket damage at this time and treat with approved methods.

Spider mites and black spot are two problems to watch for this month in ornamentals. Spider mites suck out juices from plants such as annual flowers, pyracantha, and junipers. Insecticidal soap sprays applied twice, two days apart, can help control them. Neem oil sprays should be employed regularly, especially after heavy rains. Often a sharp blast of water from a garden hose will remove aphids from most plants.

Cabbage palm caterpillars become evident in late July as they drop from palms to look for places to form cocoons. Diligently remove old palm fronds to control these insects.

Check your lawn mower blade and sharpen it if necessary. As previously mentioned, a dull blade does not cut evenly and promotes disease.

Lawns can be fertilized this month, as can citruses, fruit trees, perennial shrubs, and roses. A time-release fertilizer is best used now to provide continued nutrients as plants grow rapidly this time of year.

Harvest vegetables continually. Keeping them picked as they ripen will extend harvest times by encouraging plants to continue to produce.

Surinam cherries, mangoes, guavas, and pears begin ripening now as well. Avocados can be harvested before completely ripe and then allowed to ripen off the tree. Depending on the variety, test fruits frequently to determine proper harvest times. Mulch the area around the tree to help prevent bruising if avocados are left on the tree until completely ripe.

Mulch may need to be added to some beds in July, and should be at least three inches thick. It helps to moderate soil temperature and hold moisture. Organic mulches slowly break down, or compost, adding a small amount of nutrients to enrich the soil. Oftentimes mulching materials are free for the taking from county distribution centers or can be found within the gardener's yard.

Vegetable gardens or areas where appearances are unimportant can often be mulched with shredded newspapers or layers of whole newspapers (printed in soy inks only). Water them thoroughly after applying to keep the paper in place or tidy it up with a layer of organic mulch.

Some organic mulch materials that are usually free include:

- Pine needles
- Shredded leaves and bark
- Spanish moss

Are nematodes a problem in your garden? Solarize the soil to foil these microscopic pests that attack and damage plant roots. The process should take about four weeks and will prepare the soil for fall planting.

1. Cultivate the area of soil and cover it with clear plastic that has been effectively weighted down at the edges.
2. Keep the plastic in place for at least four weeks. Solar radiation should also destroy any weeds or other seeds or seedlings while reducing nematode populations.
3. Remove the plastic and allow the soil to air out for two weeks.
4. Add compost and other soil amendments, working them in well before planting.

A ground cover of geraniums lends an extra snap of color to this large-scale pot. Even snippets of soil can support planted areas.

Consider creating container plantings of colorful annuals and tropical perennials to brighten shady areas. Many plants prefer a location with partial to full shade at this time of year. Deadhead your flowering annuals daily to promote continual blooms.

Throughout the summer, cut back canna stems to the ground as blooms fade. Doing so keeps beds tidy and promotes new growth. Compost the stems if desired, but discard them if they show signs of disease or insect infestation. Deadhead bird-of-paradise flowers as they fade, and trim foliage to keep the clump neat.

August

Now and until the end of the hurricane season, be sure to keep shrubs and trees neatly trimmed to avoid potential storm damage. Coconuts should be removed to prevent bodily injury or property damage and you should be ready to move outdoor

Shell ginger (*Alpinia zerumbet*) needs plenty of room and is just one of the many gingers suitable for Florida gardens.

furniture, barbecue grills, sports equipment, and other items indoors when storms threaten. Preparedness is the best way to avoid possibly injury, loss, and damages.

This month is the time to start planning your fall garden. Consider having the soil tested so you'll know exactly what it does and does not need. To collect an accurate sample:

1. Take scoops of soil about three to four inches below the surface in eight different spots.
2. Mix these samples in a large bucket.
3. Measure out about a pint of the mixture and place it in a container.
4. Take this container to your county Extension office.

Order vegetable and flower seeds for your fall garden, and plant quick-growing crops of the following:

Bush bean
Lettuce
Mesclun
Spinach
Stir-fry greens

Start seedlings in flats or six-packs for cool-weather crops such as:

Broccoli
Brussels sprout
Cabbage
Cauliflower
Chard

Chinese cabbage
Collard
Kale
Lettuce
Mesclun

Tomato seedlings can be started to grow in containers through the colder months. Container culture allows tender tomato plants to be moved indoors when frost or freezing weather later threatens. Cherry tomatoes are a good choice, since they have small fruit that ripens quickly. Consistent moisture, not soggy containers, is the key to success in the container culture of tomatoes. Allowing containers to dry out may result in blossom-end rot and fruit loss. Mulch containers heavily to conserve moisture, and water and feed regularly. Once plants set fruit, stop feeding but continue the watering regimen.

Shade transplants in the garden with cuttings of small leafy branches or palmetto fronds. Just insert the stems of these cuttings into the ground near the transplants to offer midday and/or late-afternoon shade until the plants are established.

Sod webworms, army worms, chinch bugs, mole crickets, and brown-patch fungus continue to threaten lawns during August. Reducing turf areas reduces the need to treat these insect pests and diseases with pesticides and fungicides and herbicides for weeds. Reducing turf area also cuts down on mowing chores. Consider restricting turf areas to only in those frequently used places, such as play and dining areas.

∾ QUICK TIP

One Tree, One Ton

One tree can absorb one ton of carbon dioxide (the principal greenhouse gas) over its lifetime. In one year an average tree produces enough oxygen to sustain a family of four. One tree can also absorb the CO_2 output from four cars every year. Shade trees can help lower heating and cooling costs. Trees can also increase our property values, and make our neighborhoods and public spaces more attractive. Research shows that having a greener environment can even have a positive effect on our moods and our health.

Instead of grass, allow some areas to remain natural or mulch heavily and plant with native or Florida-friendly species for low-care options. (See Plate 6.)

Some perennials may become lanky now. Prune them back to encourage new growth. Poinsettias can be trimmed until the end of this month. Apply a water-soluble fertilizer after trimming.

Look for the spectacular blooms of the hurricane lily (Lycoris) this month. The sunny yellow blooms appear in August, long after the attractive foliage of these heirloom bulbs has disappeared in early summer.

September

This month is the last time to fertilize citrus trees before they go dormant for the winter. Fertilizing later could promote a fall growth spurt, which would make them susceptible to early freeze damage. Lawns can also be fertilized mid-month.

Plant strawberries this month. They will grow throughout the winter and produce in early spring.

There is still time to get in a crop of bush beans, cucumbers, and perhaps some summer squash. Lettuce, arugula, and spinach can be planted now and every two weeks thereafter for continued harvests.

September Cool-Weather Vegetables to Plant

Beet	Fava bean
Broccoli	Kale
Brussels sprout	Lettuce
Cabbage	Mesclun
Carrot	Onion
Cauliflower	Radish
Chard	Spinach
Chinese cabbage	Stir-fry greens
Collard	Turnip

Continue a watering and fertilizing regimen for orchids, according to varieties, and clivias, but begin a reduced schedule of watering and fertilizing for clivias late this month as plants go into dormancy until late spring when buds form.

❧ QUICK TIP

Saving Seeds for Love and Money

Heirloom and open pollinated vegetable and annual flowers are good subjects for seed saving. Allow some vegetables and flowers to go to seed. Collect flower seeds in envelopes, then label and seal them for planting later. Vegetable seeds should be washed with fresh water and dried on paper towels. Seal in envelope, labeling with the variety and year of collection. (See Plate 15.)

Allow papayas to ripen on the plant before harvesting. Sow papaya seeds in containers now, planting them outside in the spring when danger of frost and freezing weather has passed.

The cardboard palm (*Zamia furfuracea*), like other cycads, grows slowly, eventually forming thick clumps.

October

Satsumas begin ripening this month. These "zipper-skin" citrus fruits are often ripe and can be picked when their peels are still green. Most citrus trees will begin to enter a period of dormancy soon for the winter, although fruit will continue to ripen on the trees. Fertilizers should not be applied to citruses now through early February, though supplemental water may need to be given.

Wait until October 31 to carve that Halloween pumpkin. That way, it can still be good to cut up the following day to cook and use in holiday pies, pancakes, and spicy breads. Here are some cooking directions:

1. Wash the outside of the pumpkin before cutting. Cut pumpkin in halves or quarters to fit a roasting pan. Very large pumpkins will have to be baked in batches. Remove all seeds and scrape out filaments.

2. Place pumpkin portions in roasting pan with skin side down, adding about a cup of water to the bottom of the pan. Bake at three hundred and fifty degrees Fahrenheit for forty-five minutes or until easily pierced by a fork.

3. Remove pan from oven and allow to cool. Slice off outer skin and cut pumpkin flesh into chunks, or scoop out flesh.

4. Puree in a food processor or food mill until smooth. Place the pulp in a large strainer and allow liquid to drain off until the pulp is dense and dry (this may take several hours and a good deal of liquid will drain out). Discard liquid or add it to your compost pile along with the skin and filaments.

5. Measure out two cups and add to a zip-top freezer bag. Seal and freeze for later use.

Like little jack-o'-lanterns on a tree, Japanese persimmons begin to ripen, turning brilliant orange now. Peel and eat out of hand or puree the pulp and use it in spicy breads and cakes, or package in one-cup increments and freeze for later use. (See Plate 10.)

Snakes begin migrating to higher, drier winter hibernating locations now. Don't be surprised by them as they move through your gardens this month. Welcome their presence since they help the gardener by eating insects and other pests. Visit your local library or purchase a book on snakes so that you can positively identify your serpentine visitors.

Artistic Streak

Try sowing rye seed in patterns, such as checkerboard blocks, spirals, plaids, or rippled waves, for the fun of it. These colorful green patterns will be highlighted in a wintertime lawn.

Ryegrass can be sown now for green lawns throughout the winter. To overseed an established lawn:

1. Mow lawn short to allow seeds to reach soil.
2. Spread rye seeds at a rate of three to four pounds per one thousand square feet of lawn.
3. Water seeded areas well twice daily until seeds germinate.

Christmas cactus will bloom in time for the holidays if it gets no light from five o'clock in the afternoon to eight o'clock in the morning starting this month. Move the plant to an area with no light during those hours, returning it to its regular location during the day.

Camellias also begin blooming now depending on variety and location. Blooming continues through the winter and into March. Pyracantha displays its red berries this month, and beauty berry produces thick clusters of purple berries for wildlife (though they are toxic to humans).

White deposits around the rim of this pot are mineral buildup and indicate it is time to repot this Christmas cactus.

Ageratum

Anise hyssop

Annual phlox

Bells of Ireland

Calendula

Caladium

Carnation

Cleome

Dianthus

Larkspur

Lobelia

Nasturtium

Ornamental cabbage and kale

Petunia

Poppy

Snapdragon

Stock

Sweet pea

Zinnia

November

Many citrus varieties, such as 'Hamlin,' 'Parson Brown,' and 'Amber Sweet' juice oranges, navel oranges, Chinese honey oranges, limes, lemons, grapefruits, and satsumas are ready for picking later this month, with their fruits usually maturing gradually through this and the next couple months. Old-timers claim that it takes a bit of cold weather to sweeten the fruit. Well, that's what they say . . .

Early navel oranges can be used to make marmalade to give as a holiday gift. Production only takes a few oranges and a couple of lemons (seedless 'Meyer' lemons are a good choice) per batch. Buy a box of powdered fruit pectin, which will include a recipe. (See Plate 9.)

November Vegetables to Plant

Beet

Broccoli

Brussels sprout

Cabbage

Carrot

Cauliflower

Chard

Chinese cabbage

Collard

Fava bean

Green pea

Kale

Lettuce

Mesclun

Onion

Radish

Snow pea

Spinach

Stir-fry greens

Turnip

The brilliant yellow blooms of the cassia shrub (*Senna bicapsularis*) brighten landscapes this month, often providing plenty of flowers for holiday tables.

Spring-blooming bulbs can be planted outside now. Select only those bulbs suitable for Zones 9–10, for example: 'Texas Star' (*Narcissus x intermedius*), 'Double Roman' (*Narcissus tazetta orientalis*), 'Italicus' (*Narcissus tazetta italicus*), 'Chinese

Sacred Lily' (*Narcissus tazetta orientalis*), or grape hyacinth (*Muscari neglectum*). Plant all bulbs in a sunny location with rich, compost-amended soil at a depth of about three times the bulb diameter.

Another bulb for Florida gardeners to plant now is the rain lily. Mulch the intended beds well and, to prevent accidentally digging up the bulbs later, be sure you clearly mark planted areas to remind you of their contents.

❧ QUICK TIP

Classy Little Gift for Gardeners

Looking for a gardening gift that is big on impact and easy on the budget? Purchase a shiny garden trowel and have the recipient's name engraved on the blade—they're sure to be impressed.

Amaryllis is another spring-blooming bulb to plant outdoors now, but plant these large bulbs shallowly, with a third to half of the bulb remaining aboveground. Amaryllis bulbs are often available through mail order and can be expected to bloom in March or April.

Amaryllis bulbs already in the landscape can be prompted to bloom by withholding moisture during their winter dormancy or by digging them up in the fall, being careful not to damage or remove any of the fleshy roots. Brush soil off the roots with a soft paintbrush, remove any foliage, and place the bulbs in a shady, dry location for about seven weeks.

Then, replant the bulbs, leaving the upper third to half of the bulb aboveground.

Amaryllis is a favorite flowering bulb suitable both for potted culture and inground planting.

To have amaryllis blooms in time for the holidays, do the following:

1. Fill a six-inch terra-cotta or decorative pot about halfway full of potting soil.
2. Position the bulb in the pot, pointed end up, so that the top third of the bulb is above the rim. Add soil around bulb to fill pot.
3. Place pot in a sunny location, watering to keep soil moist but not soggy. Turn the pot if necessary to keep bloom spike growing straight. Amaryllis bulbs can be planted outside after blooming.

For spring blooms of bulbs not designated for Zones 9–11, such as daffodils or tulips, refrigerate them for six to eight weeks and then plant in planters or outside in January or February for spring blooms. Bulbs forced to produce in this manner should be discarded after blooming, as they cannot be expected to bloom again.

To force narcissus or paperwhite bulbs to bloom indoors:

1. Select a shallow container with no drainage hole.
2. Place a layer of small, clean stones or gravel in the container and position bulbs upright (pointed part up) among the stones.

Create an artful path that will allow access to all portions of the garden from rocks and old bricks set in sand.

3. Fill in with more stones and add enough water so that it touches the bottom of the bulbs.
4. Refrigerate container for three to four months as shoots and roots begin to form, watering as needed.
5. Afterwards, move the container to a sunny location and allow plants to grow and bloom, watering as needed (enough to touch roots but not bulbs).

In many areas, grass mowing needs diminish in November, although mole crickets and brown patch fungus continue to plague lawns through the fall and winter months.

Rake fallen leaves from lawns to prevent grass damage and add leaves and grass clippings to your compost pile.

November Cold-Hardy Annuals to Plant

Ageratum	Petunia
Bells of Ireland	Poppy
Carnation	Snapdragon
Larkspur	Stock
Ornamental cabbage and kale	Sweet pea
Pansy	Viola

December

Poinsettias are omnipresent in December. To keep potted plants indoors throughout the holiday season, place pots where plants will receive good light but away from heat sources and cold drafts. Water to keep plants moist but not soggy, never allowing their pots to dry out completely. Poinsettias can be planted outdoors once the weather warms.

Plant poinsettias in full sun but away from nighttime light. These plants require complete darkness at night—starting in October when flower buds are formed—in order to rebloom the following winter. Poinsettia "blooms" are actually tiny bracts located in the center of the brilliant leaves that require nighttime darkness to change color. In northern portions of the state residents should be prepared to freeze-protect these tropical plants if grown outdoors.

❧ QUICK TIP

Poinsettia Myth

Contrary to popular belief, poinsettias are not poisonous. For nearly eight decades this rumor has continued to circulate because of one unfounded story from 1919 of a child dying after eating a poinsettia leaf. Though later determined to be hearsay, the story took on a life of its own.

A live Christmas tree is a good choice, for it preserves holiday memories in a form that grows each year. In addition, a living Christmas tree can be a global present because it helps offset the effects of global warming. A living Christmas tree does require special care to ensure survival, so select a tree from a reputable local grower who can suggest a variety suitable for your area.

Types such as red cedar, sand pine, or Norfolk Island pines can make excellent holiday trees. In some cases, even carefully trimmed shrubs can be used for holiday trees. Norfolk Island pines are often used as houseplants, and should be cared for as for any houseplant. If you are selecting a balled and wrapped tree, be careful to prevent root drying. If it is cold outside, ease the tree into the warmer indoor environment by degrees, first keeping it in the garage or on an unheated porch for a couple of days.

A potted tree will need watering, but its soil should not be soggy. Because heated homes can quickly dry out a tree or force it into unseasonal growth, plan to keep it inside for no more than two weeks. Provide plenty of direct sun, and if possible, keep it away from direct heat. Do not leave a live tree lighted for more than an hour at a time.

When you are ready to plant the tree, remove all decorations and take it outside to be completely hosed to wet the foliage. Again, if there is a great temperature differential, you may need to gradually reintroduce the tree by keeping it in a garage or on a porch for a night or two before planting it outside. Remove any root wrappings and loosen roots, planting as you would any new tree or shrub.

Early settlers used what was at hand when decorating for the holidays. Local foliage from red cedar, magnolia, and palms could easily be translated into low-cost, creative decorations.

December Vegetables to Plant

Beet	Green pea
Broccoli	Kale
Brussels sprout	Lettuce
Cabbage	Mesclun
Carrot	Onion
Cauliflower	Radish
Chard	Snow pea
Chinese cabbage	Spinach
Collard	Stir-fry greens
Fava bean	Turnip

In late December many plants and shrubs will be dormant and can be safely transplanted. To prepare a very large plant or shrub for transplanting, use a shovel to cut a deep circle around it about a month before transplanting. By cutting the wide-ranging feeder roots in this manner, a new series of roots, which will help it establish, is encouraged to grow closer to the plant. When digging the plant to move it, be sure to dig a few inches past where your root-pruning cuts were made.

It is also a good idea to apply a liquid solution of root-stimulating hormone when roots are cut, using again after replantation. To transplant, prepare a hole wide and deep enough to accommodate the plant before removal to limit the time it spends out of the soil. Work some well-rotted manure or compost into the planting hole, but do not fertilize when transplanting. Always shield roots from direct sunshine, never letting them dry out.

Water well once the plant is situated, keeping it moist but not soggy until the plant is well established.

Late December is also a good time to add new perennials, shrubs, and trees to the landscape following the above planting instructions. Palm trees, however, are best planted during warmer months. Whatever the plant type, maintain a constant watering schedule for all transplants.

✑ QUICK TIP

Trees for All

Not everyone has the room or the ability to plant a tree. Even so, where there is a will, there is certainly a way. Many public botanical gardens have memoriam/honorarium programs in which individuals can sponsor special tree plantings. Another option, purchasing carbon offset credits, allows anyone to effectively plant trees, and those trees will benefit everyone through carbon sequestration, a fancy term describing carbon dioxide absorption. That's a gift for all of us.

December Cold-Hardy Annuals to Plant

Ageratum

Larkspur

Bells of Ireland

Carnation

Dianthus

Ornamental cabbage and kale

Pansy

Petunia

Poppy

Snapdragon

Stock

Sweet alyssum

Sweet pea

Viola

6

Recommended Plants

Here are some recommended annuals, perennials, vines, shrubs, and small trees to build your gardens around. Note that some plants described as annuals in other areas will become perennials in Florida's mild climate. Also, common plant names are included here because many new or casual gardeners find them more recognizable, and plant entries are listed alphabetically by common name with the scientific (Latin) name following.

Annuals

Annuals—Sun

All are suited for Zones 8 through 11, with seasonal exceptions and preferences. Look for healthy seedlings in pots or six-packs or start from seed.

African blue basil (*Ocimum kilimanscharium X basilicum purpureum*)
Height: 3'. Dark-purple foliage and purple flower spikes. Grow from seed or purchase young plants.

African mallow (*Anisodontea* spp.)
Height: 3–5'. Upright hollyhock-like growth pattern and small pink to deep-rose flowers. Grow from seed.

Agastache or anise hyssop (*A. foeniculum*)
Height: 2–4'. Lavender to purple flower spikes, though white cultivars are available. Good for use in dried arrangements and herbal teas. Easily grown from seed and may reseed itself.

Ageratum (*Ageratum houstonianum*)
Height: 4–36". Fuzzy balls of blue, lavender, white, pink, or white-mixed blooms. Good for adding winter color, but not suitable for hot and humid conditions. Grow from bedding plants.

Alyssum or sweet alyssum (*Lobularia* spp.)
Height: 3–5". Ground-hugging mounding or cascading foliage filled with tiny blooms of white, pink, purple, rose, or salmon. Many varieties are fragrant. Easily grown from seeds or bedding plants. 'Snow Princess' hybrid has larger blooms and is very fragrant.

Amaranth, especially 'Cinco de Mayo,' 'Hot Biscuits,' and 'Splendens' (*Amaranthus* spp.)
Height: 1–5'. Dramatic sprays or splashes of colored leaves and seed heads. Grow from seed or bedding plants.

Angelonia or summer snapdragon (*Angelonia augustifolia*)
Height: 2–4'. Small snapdragon-like spikes of flowers in colors ranging from white bicolors to blues and pinks. Drought tolerant. Best grown from bedding plants.

Bachelor's button or cornflower, ragged robin, hurtsickle, and other names (*Centaurea* spp.)
Height: 12". Lacy foliage and blue, white, or pink two-inch flowers. Best grown in early spring. Easy to grow from seed.

Beach sunflower (*Helianthus debilis*)
Height: 12". Small, yellow, daisy-like blooms and deep-green foliage with a low growth habit. Best in full sun. Very heat tolerant.

Begonia or wax begonia (*Begonia Semperflorens-cultorum*)
Height: 4–12". Clusters of small red to pink to white flowers and waxy green leaves. Newer hybrids offer larger blooms on bigger plants. Can also tolerate a good deal of shade. Plants tend to grow taller in shaded conditions. Grow from bedding plants. Often, these plants behave as perennials in South Florida.

Bells of Ireland (*Moluccella laevis*)
Height: 2–4'. Spikes of lime-green "cups" that are good for cutting or making dried arrangements. Easily grown from seed.

Blanket flower (*Gaillardia pulchella*)
Height: 6–24". Tough little flowering plant that withstands the worst heat, salt, and drought conditions. Often found growing wild alongside roads. Daisy-like red and yellow blooms year-round. Will reseed itself but is not invasive. Attracts butterflies. Both annual and perennial blanket flowers exist.

Brazilian snapdragon (*Otacanthus caeruleus*)
Height: 2–4'. Lavender to purple blooms that look like those of sweet peas, on upright plants. Blooms best during warmer months. Grow from bedding plants and cuttings.

Blanket flower (*Gallardia* spp.) can take the heat and humidity or drought of a Florida summer.

Bronze fennel (*Foeniculum vulgare*)
Height: 1–3'. Feathery, fragrant foliage good for back of beds. This is a medicinal herb that can also be used in salads. Good cold tolerance, and best planted in fall to early spring. Grow from seed.

Calendula or pot marigold (*Calendula officinalis*)
Height: 18". Daisy-like blooms in yellow to red. A medicinal flower with astringent properties, calendulas are good for dried arrangements and cutting. Flower petals and whole flowers can be used in herbal teas, cosmetics, and home remedies. Cold tolerant. Easily grown from seed.

Calibrachoa (*Calibrachoa* spp.)
Height: 6–10". 'Superbells' and 'Million Bells' have colorful, miniature, single petunia-like blooms that cover mounding foliage and rebloom with little deadheading necessary. Full sun with westerly protection to grow in early spring through early summer, and then again in early fall. Purchase as bedding plants. 'Double Yellow' and 'Double' varieties have double-flowering blooms.

Candytuft (*Iberis* spp.)
Height: 1'. Old-fashioned plant with upright growth and mounds of flowers in white to maroon, depending on the variety. Best grown in cold and cool months and easily started from seed.

Celosia or cock's comb (*Celosia argentea*)
Height: 4–60". Large groups of brilliantly colored, globose flowers and plumes. Pre-

fers full sun, good drainage, and low humidity. Best grown in early spring in Florida. Grow from seed or bedding plants.

Cerinthe or honeywort (*Cerinthe major*)
Height: 1'. Eye-catching blue-purple foliage of small, rounded, overlapping leaves. Good filler in cut bouquets. Best grown in cool weather with adequate moisture. Easily grown from seed.

Cleome or spider flower (*Cleome* spp.)
Height: 3–5'. Airy foliage topped with loose, large clusters of pink and white to rose blooms. Does best during cool and dry weather. Grow from seed or bedding plants. Hybrid 'Senorita Rosalita' variety is recommended.

Coleus (*Solenostemon scutellarioides*)
Height: 1–4'. Dramatically colored foliage, and new cultivars are more sun tolerant. Good for mixed containers to provide nonstop color. Flowers are insignificant and should be pinched back to keep plants from becoming leggy. Not cold tolerant. Best grown from bedding plants and cuttings which root easily in either water or potting soil. May become a perennial in some areas. (See Plate 25.)

Coreopsis or tickseed (*Coreopsis* spp.)
Height: 2–3'. Yellow daisy-like flowers. Heat and drought tolerant. Grow from seed or bedding plants.

Cosmos (*Cosmos* spp.)
Height: 2–4'. Lacy foliage and abundant, daisy-like, single, semi-double, and shell-like flowers. Colors range from solids in white to pinks to golden to red and bicolors as well. Good cold tolerance. Easily grown from seed. 'Little Ladybird' variety is recommended for container culture.

Cup and saucer or missionary bells (*Cobaea* spp.)
Length: 10'+. Robust vine with dramatic two- to three-inch-long cupped flowers in white to purple. Good support is needed for this vine as it grows quickly and can be heavy. Best grown during early spring. Grow from bedding plants or seed.

Cuphea (*Cuphea llavea*)
Height: 10–12". Shrubby growth habit with a profusion of tubular blooms, usually in reds or blues. No deadheading needed. Heat tolerant. Full sun. Best grown as bedding plants. New hybrid variety 'Totally Tempted' recommended.

Diascia (*Diascia* spp.)
Height: 6–8". Colorful new hybrids provide spikes of nonstop small blooms on compact plants. Blooms come in reds, corals, and purples. Best grown in spring through early summer from bedding plants.

Dusty miller (*Artemisia stellerana*)
Height: 6–18". Lacy, silvery foliage. Good plant for mixed containers. Dries well for everlastings and craft projects. Best purchased as bedding plants.

False Queen Anne's lace *(Ammi majus)*
Height: 2–6'. Tall plants with feathery foliage and lacy heads of tiny white flowers. Good cut flower. Try 'Green Mist' and 'White Dill.' Easily grown from seed.

Flax (*Linum* spp.)
Height: 6–18". Delicate plants with small single flowers in colors from white to blue to rose. Cold tolerant and best grown in winter. Easily grown from seed.

Horsemint (*Monarda punctata*)
Height: 8–18". Mounds of aromatic silvery-green foliage covered with dusty-pink bloom spikes in late summer. Very heat and humidity tolerant. One of the few plants to bloom in late summer. A medicinal herb, good for teas, horsemint will often reseed itself far from host plants. Grow from seed or transplant "volunteers." Horsemint can be a short-lived perennial.

Jewels of Opar (*Talinum paniculatum*)
Height: 8–12". Airy bloom heads of tiny pink flowers are held aloft a rosette of pale green ('Kingswood Gold' variety), waxy leaves. Good heat tolerance, and this plant sometimes becomes a perennial in Florida. Good filler for bouquets. Grow from seed. Partial sun to light shade preferred.

Larkspur (*Consolida ambigua*)
Height: 1–4'. Cottage-garden favorite that resembles delphinium with generally smaller plants in a range of bloom colors from white to pinks to blue to purple. Grow in winter and early spring. Larkspur is a good cut flower and can be dried for everlasting arrangements. Easily grown from seed.

Lion's tail (*Leonotis leonurus*)
Height: 3–5'. Rangy plants with spectacular, whorled, orange blooms along the stem. Very heat and drought tolerant. Start seeds in flats early in the spring for bloom in the fall. May become a perennial in some areas. (See Plate 26.)

Lisianthus (*Eustoma* spp.)
Height 6–36". Gorgeous, blousy blooms in rich colors from blues to white. Best grown from bedding plants in morning sun and afternoon shade.

Lobelia (*Lobelia* spp.)
Height: 3–10". Delicate cascading foliage packed with airy blooms in white to blues to purples. Excellent in hanging baskets and raised planters and boxes. Best grown during cool months; afternoon shade is preferred. Provide plenty of moisture, and

do not let plants dry out. Best grown from bedding plants. 'Laguna' and 'Lucia' series, 'Heavenly Lilac,' 'Dark Blue,' and 'Sky Blue' are more tolerant of heat and humidity.

Lophospermum or creeping gloxinia (*Lophospermum erubescens*)
Length. 2–6'. 'Wine Red' is a luxuriant vine with finely cut, deep-green foliage and cascades of dark-red, two-inch tubular blooms. Good for hanging baskets and window boxes. Best grown from bedding plants or potted specimens. Heat tolerant if provided adequate moisture. Attracts hummingbirds.

Love-in-a-mist (*Nigella* spp.)
Height: 1–3'. Lacy foliage and two-inch complex blooms in blues, white, or yellow. Good as a cut or dried flower with showy seedpods. Easily grown from seed.

Lysimachia or loosestrife (*Lysimachia* spp.)
Height: 12–16". 'Snow Candle' variety offers trailing spikes of tiny, pure-white blooms. May become a perennial in some areas.

Marigold (*Tagetes* spp.)
Height: 6–48". A range of bloom colors and sizes from half an inch to four inches in yellow, orange, or red, with newer near-white varieties available. Good cold and heat tolerance, though some varieties do not handle humidity well and will develop fungus and rot. Flower petals can be added to salads for color and a peppery taste. Very easily grown from seed or bedding plants.

Mecardonia (*Mecardonia* spp.)
Height: 2–3". Varieties 'Gold Flake' and 'Prima' have tiny, bright-yellow blooms and a lush, well-branched trailing habit good for container culture. No deadheading necessary. Continuously bloom and are heat tolerant.

Melampodium (*Melampodium paludosum*)
Height: 1'. An all-purpose plant that produces multitudes of small, yellow, daisy-like blooms throughout the hottest months. Tough enough to use as a ground cover in hot, sunny, and dry areas. Grow from seed or bedding plants.

Mexican mint marigold or Mexican tarragon (*Tagetes lucida*)
Height: 2'. Single, bright-yellow marigold blooms above bright-green foliage that can be used as a substitute for French tarragon. Blossoms and leaves can be used in salads or dried for herbal teas. Heat tolerant. Easily started from seed or grown from bedding plants.

Nasturtium (*Tropaeolum* spp.)
Height: 6–36". Both mounding and climbing varieties produce round, green leaves and multitudes of colorful blooms. 'Alaska' variety has variegated green-and-white

foliage. Add both leaves and blooms to salads for a peppery taste. Best grown in early spring. Easily grown from seed. 'Whirlybird' variety is good for container culture.

Nemesia (*Nemesia* spp.)
Height: 6–24". Long stems crowded with small, snapdragon-like blooms in colors from white to pinks to reds to yellows to purples to blues. Best grown from bedding plants. Recent hybrids in the 'Sunsatia' series are more heat resistant and have a showy, upright growth habit. However, all are best grown in early spring to early summer and again in fall.

Nicotiana or flowering tobacco (*Nicotiana* spp.)
Height: 2–5'. Big fuzzy leaves and clusters of two-inch tubular flowers in colors from white to pink to red to lime green (*N. langsdorffi*) that are fragrant at night. The latter is a dramatic addition to cut flower bouquets. Best grown in early spring. Easily grown from seed or bedding plants.

Ornamental cabbage and kale (*Brassica* spp.)
Height: 6–24". Brilliantly colored foliage in pinks, purples, whites, and reds mixed with various shades of green and often ruffled or pleated. Very cold tolerant. Not edible. Purchase as bedding plants or grow from seed.

Ornamental okra (*Abelmoschus* spp.)
Height: 1–7'. Large, hibiscus-like blooms in yellows, pinks, and reds. Heat tolerant. Easily grown from seed.

Ornamental pepper (*Capsicum annuum*)
Height: 4–36". Bushy plants with shiny, deep-green foliage and colorful peppers in colors from yellows to oranges to reds to purples. Especially try the 'Prairie Fire,' 'Medusa,' 'Riot,' and 'Pretty in Purple' varieties. Very heat tolerant. Best grown during warmer months. Easily grown from seed or bedding plants and are good container plants.

Ornamental sweet potato (*Ipomoea batatas*)
Length: 6–72". Colorful foliage on vining plants that provide nonstop interest in containers or beds. Can be an aggressive plant that spreads. Chartreuse, deep-red, or variegations of pale-green, pink, and white foliage distinguish this easy-to-grow plant. Grow from bedding plants or tubers. 'Desana' variety is more compact and offers several foliage color choices.

Painted tongue (*Salpiglossis* spp.)
Height: 2'. Velvety and richly colored three-inch, petunia-like flowers on upright plants. Best grown in very early spring. Easily grown from seed.

Pansy (*Viola* spp.)
Height: 6–12". The colorful, sweet faces of pansy flowers can brighten wintertime plantings. Blooms include a full range of colors as well as many variations in flower size, with some as large as four inches with ruffles and doubles. Regular deadheading prolongs bloom time, but pansies, like violas, are not tolerant of heat and humidity. Provide afternoon shade. Grow from bedding plants.

Perilla (*Perilla* spp.)
Height: 6–36". Colorful foliage plant with purple leaves. Easily grown from seed or bedding plants for garden color throughout the hottest months.

Periwinkle (*Catharanthus roseus*)
Height: 4–12". An annual that acts like a perennial, periwinkles form mounds of dark-green foliage with multitudes of five-petaled flowers in colors from white to pink to blue to apricot and variegated. Best grown in hot and dry conditions with sandy soil that gives excellent drainage. Best grown from bedding plants, though plants may reseed themselves.

Petunia, especially the 'Celebrity,' 'Daddy,' 'Mirage,' 'Pirouette,' and 'Wave' series (*Petunia* spp.)
Height: 6–36". A cool-weather garden favorite with trumpet-shaped single and double blooms in a full color range. Recent introductions include ones with miniature and cascading growth habits. Fragrance and continuous blooms are also features of some varieties. Best grown from bedding plants.

Phlox (*Phlox drummondii*)
Height: 6–12". Upright growth and clusters of small, disk-like blooms, sometimes fragrant, in a broad range of colors. Good cold resistance and best grown in winter or very early spring. Easily grown from seed.

Poppy, California variety (*Eschscholzia* spp.); or opium and Shirley varieties (*Papaver* spp.)
Height: 1–4'. Upright growth with green to gray-green foliage and single- and multiple-petal blooms in a full range of colors. Best grown from shallowly sown seed in December or January.

Portulaca, rock purslane, or moss rose (*Portulaca* spp.)
Height: 4–12". Fleshy foliage on low-growing plants with brilliantly colored, saucer-shaped flowers that last only a day. Very heat and drought tolerant, and can be grown in full sun. Does not tolerate wetness. Best grown from bedding plants, though plants will often reseed themselves.

Purple majesty (*Pennisetum glaucum*)
Height: 3–5'. Spectacular, fuzzy, purple spikes and deep-purple, corn-like foliage.

This is one of many ornamental grasses, such as 'Lime Light' spray millet and others, that are now available. Grow in beds or mixed containers. Use spikes in arrangements, or let ripen on the plant to feed wildlife. Start as seeds or grow from bedding plants.

Sage, especially *Salvia argentea*, S. Patens, 'Cambridge,' 'Salsa,' and 'Sizzler' varieties (*Salvia* spp.)
Height: 8–72". Very broad group of both annual and perennial plants that produce blooms in every color. *Salvia argentea* is a biennial that is often grown for its extremely fuzzy, large, silver-green foliage produced in its first growing season. This salvia rarely survives in Florida for a second season, during which it produces tall masses of pink blooms. There are salvias for every condition and use in the garden—provided there is adequate sun. Depending on variety, grow from seed, cuttings, or bedding plants. Some types have flower and foliage fragrances that would not be described as pleasant.

Scaevola (*Scaevola aemula*)
Length: 18". Cascading growth habit with one-inch, fan-like blooms in blues and purples. Great heat tolerance and a good choice for hanging baskets and window boxes. Best grown from bedding plants.

Scoparia (*Scoparia* spp.)
Height: 1'. 'Lemon Mist' variety produces a mound of finely cut, medium-green foliage with a red licorice scent and a continuous abundance of dainty (half-inch), star-shaped yellow flowers. Heat tolerant.

Snapdragon (*Antirrhinum* spp.)
Height: 8–36". Full floral spikes with blooms in a wide range of colors and variegations. Good cut flower and excellent annual for cooler seasons. Easily grown from seed or bedding plants.

Statice (*Limonium sinuatum*)
Height: 1–2'. Clusters of papery blooms (good for dried arrangements) in white, yellows, pinks, blues, rose, and purples. Very slug-resistant plants. Grow from seed or bedding plants.

Stock (*Matthiola* spp.)
Height: 8–18". Fragrant clusters of blooms on upright plants. Flower colors range from white to pinks to reds to purples. Easily grown from seed.

Sunflower (*Helianthus* spp.)
Height: 1–10'. Large, single or multiple flowers on strong stalks. Many colors available from pale white to deep burgundy with single to multiple blooms. Miniature

varieties such as 'Junior,' 'Baby Bear,' 'Knee High,' and 'Music Box' are recommended for container culture. Full sun. Very easily grown from seed.

Sutera or bacopa (*Sutera* spp.)
Length: 2'. Cascading growth habit and a multitude of small, half-inch blooms in blue, white, yellow, pink, violet, lavender, or red with dainty foliage make this a good choice for container culture and hanging planters. Good heat and drought tolerance. Full sun. Best grown from bedding plants.

Sweet pea (*Lathyrus odoratus*)
Length: 1–10'. Fragrant, two- to three-inch blooms in a full range of colors and bi-colors on climbing vines with bluish-green foliage. Excellent cut flower. Start seeds in the ground in December and provide a trellis or other structure on which vines can climb. Some new varieties are bush-like and need no staking. Very cold toler-ant. The heirloom variety 'Cupid' is a good choice for container culture. All types are inedible.

Torenia or wishbone flower (*Torenia flava, T. fournieri*)
Height: 1'. Compact plant with curious and attractive trumpet-shaped blooms in velvety yellows, purples, white, and pinks. Best grown in early spring as plants get leggy as heat increases, though some hybrids in the 'Catalina' and 'Summer Wave' series offer better heat tolerance. Best grown from bedding plants in sun or partial shade.

Verbena, especially *Verbena bonariensis* and other hybrids (*Verbena* spp.)
Height: 8–36". Wide variety of growth patterns from spreading to mounding vari-eties, from the bedding verbenas, which come in many rich colors, to the tall and airy purple *V. bonariensis*. *Verbena bonariensis* can often be found growing along roadsides, and is considered perennial although it rarely survives in the garden for more than one season. Good drought and heat tolerance, though best planted in early spring. Grow from seed or bedding plants.

Viola, Johnny-jump-up, or heart's-ease (*Viola* spp.)
Height: 6–12". Delicate and colorful, violas are great wintertime container plants used on their own or in mixed plantings. Bloom colors range across the full spec-trum with bicolors and variations. Regular deadheading will extend bloom time, but usually plants are intolerant of heat and humidity. The 'Sorbet' series offers better heat tolerance. May need sun protection in afternoons. Grow from bedding plants.

Wax begonia or begonia (*Semperflorens-cultorum*)
Height: 6–12". (See Annuals—Sun section entry.)

Zinnia (*Zinnia* spp.)
Height: 6–48". Old-fashioned favorite that can be difficult in humid conditions, but certainly heat tolerant. Try 'Profusion,' 'Profusion Double,' and 'Zahara' series for disease resistance. Makes a great cut or dried flower. Grow from seed, starting plants in late winter for late spring flowering, or use bedding plants.

Annuals—Shade

Begonia or wax begonia (*Begonia Semperflorens-cultorum*)
Height: 6–12". (See Annuals—Sun section entry.)

Browallia or bush violet (*Browallia americana* and *Browallia speciosa*)
Height: 1–3'. One of the best blue blossoms for shaded locations, this plant also offers purple, violet, or blue-and-white two-inch, petunia-like blooms. Prefers morning sun with filtered shade thereafter. This delicate plant will reseed itself and in some areas has naturalized, but is not aggressive.

Coleus (*Solenostemon scutellarioides*)
Height: 1–4'. (See Annuals—Sun section entry.)

Impatiens (*Impatiens walleriana*)
Height: 1–2'. Glossy green foliage and abundant single or double blooms in colors from white to pink to red and variegations with thirty or more colors available. Heat tolerant and perennial in many areas. Plants spread by seeds and cuttings which root easily in water or potting soil. Grow from bedding plants. Some hybrids tolerate full sun. Hybrids in the 'Rockapulco' series offer double, rose-like blooms in pinks, reds, and white. The 'Dazzler' series has coral or white blooms with good branching and dark foliage.

New Guinea impatiens (*Impatiens hawkeri*)
Height: 1–2'. Bushy plants with very dark, glossy green, variegated or bronze foliage and dramatic single blooms of up to three inches in diameter displaying brilliant colors from white to pink to lilac and orange to deep reds. Provide adequate moisture and good drainage. Not cold tolerant. Grow from bedding plants.

Pansy (*Viola* spp.)
Height: 6–12". (See Annuals—Sun section entry.)

Persian shield (*Strobilanthes* spp.)
Height: 3'. Intricate, purple-patterned foliage with dramatic six- to nine-inch leaves provides color in sunny locations with some afternoon shade. Pinch plants back to keep the foliage bushy. This plant often becomes perennial in Florida, although it requires cold protection. Grow from seed, bedding plants, or by cuttings.

Torenia or wishbone flower (*Torenia flava, T. fournieri*)
Height: 1'. (See Annuals—Sun section entry.)

Viola, Johnny-jump-up, or heart's-ease (*Viola* spp.)
Height 6–12". (See Annuals—Sun section entry.)

Perennials

Perennials—Sun

African iris (*Dietes iridioides*)
Zones 8–11. Height: 2–3'. Strappy foliage with two- to three-inch blooms in either white with blue-and-yellow centers or yellow with rust centers. Very heat and drought tolerant, blooming throughout the warmer months. Divide clumps for more plants. 'Katrina' variety has full, white blooms with yellow-orange centers and bright-green foliage with increased tolerance of heavy, poorly drained soil.

Agapanthus or lily of the Nile (*Agapanthus* spp.)
Zones 8–11. Height: 2–3'. A rhizomatous evergreen with strap-like foliage and tall clusters of deep- to pale-blue or white flowers in late spring or early summer. Can tolerate some shade. Drought and heat tolerant. Can be divided. (See Plate 3.)

Agave (*Agave* spp.)
Zones 8–11. Height: 1–20'. Large group of slow-growing succulent plants that are very drought, salt, and heat tolerant. Dwarf varieties are good sculptural additions to the landscape. Varieties such as 'Spot,' with purple blotches on silvery-green leaves, provide color interest as well. These plants make good container specimens. Some are extremely cold tolerant.

Aloe (*Aloe* spp.)
Zones 9–11. Height: 1–4'. A group of sculptural, succulent plants with lance-like leaves and a compact growth pattern. Some, such as the popular Barbados aloe, bloom with tall spikes of color, usually yellows to reds. Extremely drought, heat, and salt tolerant. Provide good drainage. Aloes exist for both sunny and shady gardens. Cold tolerance depends on variety.

Amaryllis (*Hippeastrum* spp.)
Zones 9–11. Height: 1–4'. Wide variety of bloom colors and combinations, including dwarf, double, and single, with large, bell-shaped, five- to eight-inch dramatic flowers. Bulbs bloom in the spring atop sturdy stalks over strap-like green foliage.

Aloe (*Aloe* spp.) is both heat and drought tolerant.

Aztec lily or Jacobean lily (*Sprekelia* spp.)
Zones 8–10. Height 5–18". Orchid-like crimson flowers on ten- to eighteen-inch stems in summer. Strap-like green foliage.

Begonia (*Begonia* spp.)
Zones 8–11. Height: 6–60". A wide variety of tender plants including rex and rhizomatous, all of which have dramatic foliage. Many varieties with brilliant leaf colors. 'Dragon Wing' variety displays profuse clusters of small, brilliant blooms in red or orange. 'Bellagio' and 'Mandalay' hybrids offer large, double blooms in lush colors. Rhizomatous begonias, such as the lily pad, produce some of the largest leaves, reaching up to two feet in diameter. All are tropical plants that need cold protection. Provide good light but plenty of shade and drainage. Allow these varieties to dry out before watering.

Bird-of-paradise (*Strelitzia* spp.)
Zones 9–11. Height: 3–4'. Good in full sun to light shade with large, deep-green leaves and exotic orange (*Strelitzia reginae*) or white (*Strelitzia alba*) bird-like flowers in late summer or fall. White varieties grow up to eighteen feet. Needs cold protection.

Blackberry lily (*Belamcanda chinensis*)
Zones 8–11. Height: 2–3'. Iris-like green foliage with branched spikes of numer-

ous orange to yellow blooms. Its name comes from the black seeds visible when seedpods split. Drought and cold tolerant. Plants will multiply and reseed and can be divided.

Blood lily (*Scadoxus multiflorus*)
Zones 9–10. Height: 10–14". Bright-red and striking, six-inch spheres atop sturdy stalks in the summer. Attractive, broad, lance-shaped leaves emerge after blooms on this heirloom bulb plant.

Blue daze (*Evolvulus glomeratus*)
Zones 9–11. Height: 6–10". Nonstop small blue blooms distinguish this perennial, which makes a good ground cover. Salt, heat, and drought tolerant. Root cuttings for more plants.

Bulbine (*Bulbine frutescens*)
Zones 8–11. Height: 6–18". Succulent, long leaves and spikes of small orchid-like blooms in yellows and oranges throughout the summer. Very heat and drought tolerant. Spreads slowly and can be divided. Provide good drainage.

Caladium (*Caladium* spp.)
Zones 8–11. Height: 6–36". Large, heart-shaped leaves grown from perennial corms for their spectacular color combinations, which include reds, pinks, whites, greens, and chartreuse. Some varieties are best grown in shade, while others are more suited to sunny beds. Good container specimen with heat tolerance. In northern zones, dig tubers in fall and store them over winter. Replant in late spring.

Calla lily (*Zantedeschia* spp.)
Zones 8–10. Height: 1–2'. Large, trumpet-shaped flowers in white, yellow, red, or pink with deep-green foliage that becomes dormant after flowering. Partial sun and rich soil are preferred. Mulch well in North Florida for cold protection of the tender tubers. 'Edge of Night' variety produces dramatic, dark-purple blooms and purple-edged foliage.

Cat's whiskers (*Orthosiphon stamineus*)
Zones 9–11. Height: 2–3'. Shrubby perennial with showy white or lavender blooms that have very long stamens (hence the "whiskers") throughout the year. Needs cold protection.

Coleus (*Solenostemon scutellarioides*)
Height: 1–4'. (See Annuals—Sun section entry.)

Crinum lily (*Crinum* spp.)
Zones 8–11. Height: 2–8'. Flowering bulbs with clusters of large, fragrant, white,

pink, rose, or striped trumpet-shaped blooms on spikes that range from two to four feet above strap-like foliage. 'Queen Emma' crinum (*C. procerum*, var. *splendens*)has maroon leaves and grows to five feet or more. Partial sun is preferred.

Crocosmia (*Crocosmia montbretia*)
Zones 8–10. Height: 1–3'. Flowering bulbs that produce strap-like foliage and spikes of yellow to red blooms. Can be grown in partial shade. Very cold tolerant.

Daylily (*Hemerocallis* spp.)
Zones 8–10. Height 1–3'. Green, strap-like foliage that forms a clump. Large, trumpet-shaped blooms in late spring. The plant lies dormant in most areas during winter months. Many cultivars available in a variety of colors and bloom configurations ranging from near-white to yellows, oranges, and reds. Morning sun and afternoon shade preferred. Grow in rich soil with adequate moisture. Keep beds weed-free.

Devil's backbone (*Pedilanthus tithymaloides*)
Zones 9–11. Height: 2–3'. Variegated waxy foliage in pale green and white with pink accents make this upright plant stand out in landscapes and container plantings. Needs cold protection. Suitable for sun or shade.

Fairy bells (*Disporum cantoniense*)
Zones 7–10. Height: 3'. Grow this Chinese species of fairy bells in partial sun to shade. Three-foot, bamboo-like shoots rise in early spring, often with a purple tint as they emerge and unfurl into a multibranched clump, topped in late spring with dazzling, dark-purple, bell-like flowers.

False dragonhead or obedient plant (*Physostegia virginiana*)
Zones 8–9. Height: 6–24". Pink, white, or lilac bloom spikes on low growth in the late summer. Spreads by runners, but varieties such as 'Summer Snow' and 'Miss Manners' do not spread readily. Good cold tolerance.

Firecracker plant or coral plant (*Russelia equisetiformis*)
Zones 8–11. Height: 1–3'. Bright-red, tubular blooms appear profusely on delicate foliage with a cascading growth habit. Attractive to hummingbirds and butterflies. Provide cold protection.

Flax lily (*Daniella tasmanica variegata*)
Zones 8–10. Height: 1–3'. A variegated grass for full sun or shaded areas. This and the other *Daniella* cultivars produce airy panicles of often blue blooms in the winter or early spring, followed by small blue berries. Easily divided, they are a nice ground cover and are heat and drought tolerant. 'Tasred' cultivar has bright green and red strap-like foliage.

Flax lily (*Daniella tasmanica variegata*) offers drought- and heat-tolerant foliage and airy blue blossoms.

Flowering maple (*Abutilon* spp.)
Zones 8–10. Height: 2–20'. Shrubby plant with dramatic, hibiscus-like blooms in colors ranging from yellow to orange to rose to white. Provide filtered sun with afternoon shade.

Geranium (*Pelargonium* spp.)
Zones 8–11. Height: 6–36". Wide variety of shrubby plants with often colorful and fuzzy leaves, including many fragrant-leaved varieties such as rose, lemon, or apple-scented types which usually have insignificant flowers. Others, such as 'Black Magic Rose,' are grown for their prolific and colorful heads of blooms in colors from rose to pink to reds to whites. Tolerates heat well, but does poorly in humid conditions. Good container or bedding plants for winter and spring culture. Scented varieties make good ground cover. Most root well from cuttings in potting soil. May need cold protection in some areas.

Grape hyacinth (*Muscari neglectum*)
Zones 8–10. Height: 6". A strong Southern strain with small, bluish-purple flowers appearing two to three inches above a small fountain of grass-like foliage. Blooms in

late February or early March. It can reproduce by seed, allowing it to naturalize. This bulb often spreads across yards over a period of years, and can serve as a graceful border at the base of deciduous trees. As a good rule of thumb, as with most bulbs, plant at a depth about three times the height of the bulb.

Horsemint or spotted bee balm (*Monarda punctata*)
Zones 8–10. Height: 8–18". (See Annuals—Sun section entry.)

Jacobinia, Brazilian plume, flamingo flower, or pineapple geranium (*Justicia carnea*)
Zones 8–11. Height: 4'. Very showy bright-pink pom-poms atop deep, crinkly, green foliage. Upright growth habit that may require staking and benefits from heavy pruning. Makes an excellent cut flower. May need cold protection. Cuttings root easily in potting soil. Other varieties have white, yellow, or orange blooms. (See Plate 24.)

Jerusalem sage (*Phlomis* spp.)
Zones 8–10. Height: 24–30". Felt-like, gray-green foliage and tall spikes with whorls of snapdragon-like flowers in yellow. Plants spread to form clumps. Hybrids include: 'Miss Grace' (*Phlomis fruticosa*), 'Balearic Island Phlomis' (*Phlomis italica*), and 'Edward Bowles'. Drought tolerant. Grow in full to partial sun.

Kalanchoe (*Kalanchoe* spp.)
Zones 8–11. Height: 6–24". A large family of plants with fleshy, succulent foliage. Forms several brilliant clusters of tiny, star-shaped blooms in reds, pinks, oranges, and yellows. *Kalanchoe thyrsiflora* is grown for its distinctive foliage, which consists of large, fleshy leaves tipped with crimson and arranged in a flower-like rosette. Very heat and drought tolerant and has a long bloom period. Tolerates poor soils, but needs cold protection. Root cuttings in potting soil, or grow from bedding plants.

Lantana (*Lantana* spp.)
Zones 8–11. Height: 1–5'. This plant is listed with reservation. Some species (*Lantana campara*, for instance) are very aggressive or invasive, but because of its ability to bloom despite heat and humidity, cultivars such as 'Samantha,' with its variegated foliage and butter-yellow blooms, 'Purple Trailing,' 'Gold Mound,' 'Morning Glow,' 'Radiation,' 'Sonset,' 'Miss Huff,' 'Ham and Eggs,' or 'Star Landing' make good ground covers and container plants. Other recommended hybrids include 'Grape,' 'Lemonade,' 'Luscious,' 'Citrus Blend,' and 'Tropical Fruit.' In addition, many butterflies and hummingbirds love lantana. Heat and drought tolerant. Grow in full sun. Trimming seed heads can help prevent the spread of more aggressive varieties.

Lavender (*Lavendula* spp.)
Zones 8–9. Height: 6–24". Fragrant, gray-green foliage with a mounding growth habit and small lavender blooms distinguish this garden herb. A short-lived perennial, lavender is heat tolerant, but does poorly in very humid or wet conditions.

Dry leaves and buds for sachets and herbal teas. Grow from seed, root cuttings, or bedding plants.

Lemongrass (*Cymbopogon* spp.)
Zones 8–11. Height: 3–6'. Attractive grass and culinary herb with a citrus/lemon fragrance and flavor. Needs cold protection in Zones 8 and 9.

Lion's tail (*Leonotis leonurus*)
Zones 8–11. Height: 3–5'. (See Annuals—Sun section entry.)

Louisiana iris (*Iris* spp.)
Zones 8–10. Height: 2–3'. (See Native Plants section entry.)

Lycoris or hurricane or spider lily (*Lycoris* spp.)
Zones 8–10. Height: 1–4'. Funnel-shaped flowers, four inches wide, that bloom in late summer. Related to amaryllis. Prefers alkaline soil. Strap-like green foliage is dormant in summer, but appears following bloom time in late summer. Varieties include: golden spider lily (*Lycoris aurea*), with golden-yellow flower clusters, spider lily (*Lycoris radiata*), with crimson flower clusters, magic or nekkid ladies lily (*Lycoris squamigera*), with rose-pink bloom clusters tinged with amethyst, and tie-dye surprise lily (*Lycoris sprengeri*), with dark-pink flower clusters. Very cold and drought tolerant. A valuable, old-fashioned, Southern bulb flower that spreads slowly by division. Bulbs can attain very large sizes. Grow in full sun to partial shade.

Maiden grass (*Miscanthus* spp.)
Zones 8–10. Height: 3–4'. Upright structural grass with horizontal bands of gold on emerald blades. Compact, dwarf growth habit. Burgundy flower heads appear in late summer. Provide afternoon sun protection. 'Little Zebra' is a variegated choice.

Mexican heather (*Cuphea hyssopifolia*)
Zones 8–11. Height: 1–2'. Mounding, shrub-like growth habit on compact plants with small leaves and tiny lavender or white blooms. Needs cold protection. Cuttings can be rooted and the plant will often reseed itself, but is not invasive. 'Bat Face' variety (*Cuphea llavea*) has striking and profuse deep-red and purple blooms and grows to be a small, shrubby, semi-sprawling plant that is one to two feet tall.

Mondo grass (*Ophiopogon japonicus*)
Zones 8–10. Height: 6–12". Broad blades of grass create a thick clump of growth. Dwarf species have more delicate foliage. Also, variegated selections and most other varieties produce spikes of small purple or lavender blooms. Very drought and shade tolerant. All are good ground covers and edging material. 'Nigrescens' variety has nearly black foliage and is good in containers. 'Super Dwarf' grows to only one inch tall. Prefers partial sun to shade.

Narcissus, 'Texas Star' variety (*Narcissus x intermedius*)
Zones 8–10. Height: 1'. The toughest of the jonquil hybrids, this plant performs well in clay, sand, and even dry ground, with slightly curved foliage and sweet fragrance. The flowers are vibrant yellow cups with yellow petals. Plant bulbs from early September to late November in an area that gets half a day of winter sun. Blooms in early spring. Other narcissus varieties suitable for Zones 8–10 include: 'Italicus,' 'Double Roman,' 'Grand Primo' (*Narcissus tazetta*), 'Chinese Sacred Lily' (*Narcissus tazetta orientalis*), and 'Twin Sisters' (*Narcissus x medioluteus*). As a good rule of thumb for most bulbs, plant at a depth about three times the height of the bulb.

New Zealand flax (*Phormium* spp.)
Zones 8–10. Height: 4–6'. Handsome grass-like growth with wide blades of foliage and airy blooms. 'Pink Stripe' variety produces an erect rosette of stiff, olive-green, strap-like foliage with vivid pink margins. 'Yellow Wave' has softer, arching foliage that emerges a pale yellow and develops into green stripes. Some thirty varieties available. Grow in full sun with well-drained, rich soil and adequate moisture.

Papyrus (*Cyperus papyrus*)
Zones 8–11. Height: 1–5'. Numerous water plants with long, slender, straight stems with tufts of leaves on top. 'Viviparus' (*Cyperus haspan*) is a dwarf variety that is about one foot tall. 'Baby Tut' (*Cyperus involucratus*) grows to two feet and 'King Tut' (*Cyperus papyrus*) grows to six feet. Full sun to partial shade in water gardens and ponds.

Pentas (*Pentas lanceolata*)
Zones 8–10. Height: 1–3'. Mounded growth habit, deep green foliage, and large clusters of small, star-shaped flowers in reds, pinks, white, blues, and purples. Very dependable plant with a long bloom period. Attracts butterflies.

Periwinkle or vinca (*Catharanthus roseus*)
Zones 8–11. Height: 2'. Glossy green foliage, mounding growth habit, and nonstop disk-like blooms from white to purples. Prefers full sun. Very heat, drought, and somewhat salt tolerant. Will reseed itself, but not aggressively.

Philippine violet (*Barleria cristata*)
Zones 8–11. Height 3–4'. Upright, shrubby plant with small lavender blooms. Prune hard to maintain plant shape. Tolerates shade and is drought tolerant. *Barleria repens* is an aggressive species that can spread rapidly.

Pineapple lily (*Eucomis* spp.)
Zones 8–11. Height: 3'. 'Sparkling Burgundy' cultivar has eye-catching, deep-purple, strap-like leaves on a barrel-shaped spike. Flowers in late summer to early fall.

Plectranthus (*Plectranthus* spp.)
Zones 9–11. Height: 1–5'. Wide variety of low-growing and bushy perennials grown for their showy spikes of tubular blooms in blue, pink, lavender, or white, plus variegated foliage. Relatives of that old houseplant standby, Swedish ivy, these plants are right at home in Florida gardens. Good choices include 'Creeping Coleus' (*Plectranthus madagascariensis*), Cuban oregano (*Plectranthus amboinicus*), and 'Purple Smelly Dog Plant' (*Plectranthus ecklonii*). Some will need cold protection.

Porterweed or false vervain, blue snakeweed, or Jamaica vervain (*Stachytarpheta jamaicensis*)
Zones 8–11. Height: 7'. Attains the stature of a small shrub, but can be trimmed to keep growth in check. Blooms are rattails of blue, purple, or salmon that travel up the six-inch spike over time. Odoriferous green foliage. Great heat, humidity, and drought tolerance. Its rampant growth rate makes it a dubious recommendation for some areas. Grow from cuttings or bedding plants. Attracts butterflies.

Pratia (*Pratia angulata*)
Zones 8–10. Height: 1". Ground cover with zigzag black stems clothed in tiny round leaves that form a nice mat topped with small, lobelia-like, white flowers from late spring through early summer. Tolerant of wet conditions. Partial sun preferred.

Rain lily or fairy or zephyr lily (*Zephyranthes* spp.)
Zones 8–11. Height: 1'. (See Native Plants section entry.)

Ribbon fern or Hawaiian ribbon fern (*Pteris cretica*)
Zone 8–10. Height: 2'. Dark-green, ribbon-like leaves. The common ribbon fern is believed to be native to Florida, as some botanists insist that a stand found in the Florida panhandle just north of Marianna is a native one. 'Ping Wu' dwarf hardy ribbon fern (*Pteris cretica*) forms a one-foot-tall plant with very narrow fronds. 'Western Hills' hardy ribbon fern (*Pteris cretica var. nervosa*) is a vigorous grower that can create a five-foot-wide-by-three-foot-tall, deciduous clump of light-green leaves that resemble very long fingers. In early fall, the fertile fronds arise like a flagpole from the center of the clump. All prefer partial sun to light shade.

Rosemary (*Rosmarinus officinalis*)
Zones 8–11. Height: 6–24". Aromatic, silvery-green foliage and bushy growth habit. It can be trimmed to form a low hedge or as a potted topiary. Use its fragrant leaves in cooking. Very heat and drought tolerant, though it performs poorly in humid/wet conditions. May need cold protection.

Sage (*Salvia* spp.)
Zones 8–11. Height: 1–5'. Wide range of both annual and perennial plants, some of which grow quite large and flower year-round. Flower colors include the whole

range, with some of the best and deepest true blues to be found. Hummingbird or Texas sage (*Salvia coccinea*) has red blooms that attract hummingbirds and butterflies and will often reseed itself in the landscape. The desirable, foot-long, pale-yellow bloom spikes of forsythia sage are produced in late summer through fall. Some of the perennial salvias grow quickly and may require frequent pruning to maintain shape, but they are worth the effort for their spectacular blooms. Most perennial salvias root well from cuttings. All prefer a sunny location.

Shrimp plant (*Justicia brandegeana*)
Zones 8–11. Height: 4'. Rangy plant with showy blooms that resemble shrimp throughout spring to fall. Flower colors vary from reds ('Jambalaya') to pinks to yellows ('Yellow Queen'), depending on variety. Tolerates some shade and requires cold protection. Great hummingbird and butterfly plant. Divide or take root cuttings for more plants. Yellow shrimp plant (*Pachystachys lutea*), also called lollipop plant, can be grown in partial shade and has an upright growth habit. It is suitable for Zones 9–11.

Society garlic (*Tulbaghia violacea*)
Zones 8–11. Height: 1'. Thick grass-like clumps produce clusters of lavender-pink blooms throughout the summer. Tolerates heat and humidity. Is a member of the onion family. Slow to spread by bulb division.

Southern fall crocus or autumn crocus, autumn daffodil, or winter daffodil (*Sternbergia lutea* spp.)
Zones 8–10. Height: 6". A native of Greece, this is a good bulb for rock gardens with low blooming habit and foliage that requires little maintenance. Prefers good drainage and slightly gravelly/acidic sandy loam to slightly alkaline clay soils. Can be found naturalized in heavy, black soils that tend to dry out and crack during summer months. Yellow, crocus-like blooms appear in the fall.

Spider brake fern (*Pteris multifida*)
Zones 8–10. Height: 1'. Narrow, skeleton-like, thick green leaves forming an eighteen-inch-wide clump. Naturalizes in mortar joints and rock walls and prefers alkaline conditions. A very easy fern for a sunny garden location where a "ferny" texture is needed. Full to partial sun is preferred.

Texas ageratum (*Eupatorium greggii*)
Zones 8–10. Height: 2'. Grow in full to partial sun. Begins to flower in September and continues into December. The three-foot-wide, slowly spreading mound of light-green foliage is covered in fall with two-inch clusters of airy, blue-violet flowers.

Tiger grass (*Thysanolaena maxima*)
Zones 9–11. Height: 10'. The look of bamboo in a grass that can tolerate a good

deal of shade. Excellent container plant for a tropical look and wet areas. Provide adequate moisture. Needs cold protection in Zone 9.

Verbena (*Verbena* spp.)
Zones 8–10. Height: 4–48". Perennial varieties include a low-growing hybrid that is useful for ground cover in northern portions of the state, producing a range of colored bloom heads from white to red to purple. Upright verbena has four-foot-long, white bloom spikes that attract butterflies. Bloom time for most is early spring.

Walking iris (*Neomarica* spp.)
Zones 9–11. Height: 2–3'. Both the white- and yellow-flowered varieties exhibit the interesting habit of self-propagation by forming plantlets at the tips of their strap-like leaves; these plantlets take root as the leaves droop down to touch the ground. Makes a nice hanging basket specimen but can be rather sparse in a landscape since it does not form clumps as do most irises.

Whirling butterflies or wand flowers (*Gaura lindheimeri*)
Zones 8–9. Height: 1–3'. Mounded growth habit with many delicate white/pink single blooms from spring through fall. Variegated forms have pink flowers and variegated leaves.

Perennials—Shade

Alocasia (*Alocasia* spp.)
Zones 10–11. Height: 1–8'. Large group of evergreen plants, most grown for their dramatic foliage. *Alocasia plumbea* produces huge leaves on tall stalks growing up to eight feet. 'New Guinea Gold' (*Alocasia macrorrhiza*) grows to fifteen feet and has bright-yellow stalks and leaf veins, while *Alocasia x amazonica* has deeply serrated leaves veined with white and grows one to two feet tall. 'Black Velvet' is a dwarf variety with chalky, blackish leaves that are green to black with distinct, light veining. 'Cuprea' has ten- to fourteen-inch-wide, glossy, metallic-looking copper leaves with brilliant purple undersides. All prefer bright, filtered light and well-drained, rich organic soils with adequate moisture. In colder zones, grow these handsome plants in containers to bring under cover during colder months. Container culture will help reduce the chance that these plants will spread wildly.

Aloe (*Aloe* spp.)
Zones 9–11. Height: 1–4'. (See Perennials-Sun section entry.)

Aluminum plant, friendship plant, artillery plant, or creeping Charlie (*Pilea* spp.)
Zones 9–11. Height: 1–2'. Variegated, coin-shaped, silver/green leaves on a spreading plant that forms a ground cover in shaded areas. May die back after frost, but will return.

Amazon lily or eucharis lily (*Eucharis amazonica*)
Zones 10–11. Height: 1'. Evergreen bulbs with clusters of white, lightly fragrant, daffodil-like blooms, about three inches wide and nodding. Forms thick clumps in moist, fertile soils. Prefers bright shade to filtered sun.

Anthurium or flamingo flowers (*Anthurium* spp.)
Zones 10–11. Height: 1–3'. Several species and hybrids (five hundred or more) grown for their showy spathes that appear in summer months, and some for their intricate leaves. All require shade and rich organic soils for best performance.

Begonia or angel wing or cane begonia (*Begonia x argenteo-guttata*)
Zones 9–11. Height: 2–4'. Dramatically spotted and colored, pointed, and ruffled leaves. Some varieties produce mounds of brilliant blooms from scarlet to orange to pinks and white. Not cold hardy, though many types tolerate more sunshine than do the rex varieties. Allow soil to dry completely before watering. *Begonia boliviensis/tuberous-cross*, 'Mandalay' (single-flowered) and 'Bellagio' (double-flowered), produce huge, pendulous blooms on cascading foliage.

Begonia, rex type (*Begonia rex-cultorum*)
Zones 9–11. Height: 1–3'. Some varieties, such as the lily pad begonia, have dramatic, full leaves, and many produce showy clusters of blooms. Truly shade-loving, these tropical plants prefer hot and humid conditions but will not tolerate consistently wet soil. Allow soil to dry completely before watering. Need cold protection when temperatures are below fifty-five degrees Fahrenheit. 'Phoe's Cleo,' 'Metallic Mist,' and 'Fireworks' varieties display dramatically patterned foliage.

Blue ginger (*Dichorisandra thyrsiflora*)
Zones 8–11. Height: 1–3'. Not a true ginger, this plant is a relative of common spiderwort. Attractive spikes of blue blooms are produced in early summer through fall. The plant dies back in colder areas, but will reemerge in spring.

Bromeliad (*Aechmea* spp., *Cryptanthus* spp., *Guzmania* spp., *Neoregelia* spp., and *Vriesea* spp.)
Zones 9–11. Height: 1–5'. A broad group of plants with stiff leaves that form rosette clumps, often creating moisture reservoirs. Bromeliads are grown for both their showy bloom spikes and colorful, sculptural leaves. Some, such as *Vriesia imperialis*, grow to the gargantuan proportions of nearly five feet tall and five to seven feet in diameter, while some *Cryptanthus* species (see the earth star entry below, for instance) are but two inches tall. Some bromeliads are terrestrial and others are epiphytic. Most require shade, especially those that grow on large oak trees, and terrestrial varieties prefer a rich organic soil. (See Plate 5.)

Caladium (*Caladium* spp.)
Zones 8–11. Height: 6–36". (See Perennials—Sun section entry.)

Cast-iron plant (*Aspidistra elatior*)
Zones 8–11. Height: 2–3'. Attractive, evergreen, paddle-shaped, two- to three-foot-long leaves form clusters of deep-green, yellow-green, variegated-striped, or even spotted patterns. A plant that can add interest to shaded locations. Excellent drought tolerance. 'China Moon' variety has medium-green leaves spotted with yellow.

Clivia (*Clivia miniata*)
Zones 9–11. Height: 2–3'. Evergreen, strap-like foliage that forms clumps and exceptional clusters of orange to yellow to creamy white blooms in late winter to early spring. Restrict watering during cold months and resume in the spring when buds appear. Will need cold protection in Zone 9, where it is best grown as a container specimen. Plants prefer crowded conditions.

Coleus (*Solenostemon scutellarioides*)
Zones 8–11. Height: 1–4'. (See Annuals—Sun section entry.)

Crinum lily (*Crinum* spp.)
Zones 8–11. Height: 2–8'. (See Perennials—Sun section entry.)

Crossandra (*Crossandra infundibuliformis*)
Zones 9–11. Height: 1–4'. Mounds of crinkly green foliage with profuse bloom clusters of red, orange, or yellow. Needs cold protection in Zone 9. Cuttings can be rooted for more plants. Filtered sun with afternoon shade preferred.

Crinum lilies (*Crinum* spp.) can form large clumps and bloom from spring through fall.

Daylily (*Hemerocallis* spp.)
Zones 8–10. Height: 1–4'. (See Perennials—Sun section entry.)

Devil's backbone (*Pedilanthus tithymaloides*)
Zones 9–11. Height: 2–3'. (See Perennials—Sun section entry.)

Earth stars (*Cryptanthus* spp.)
Zones 8–11. Height 2–10". Diminutive and colorful, earth stars are tiny rosettes with stiff, striped, spotted, or banded leaves that often have undulating edges. Excellent, slowly spreading ground cover plant. Require good drainage but constant moisture. Actually a bromeliad with possibly thousands of hybrids.

Foxtail fern (*Asparagus meyeri*)
Zones 8–11. Height: 1–2'. Bushy spikes of evergreen, pale-green foliage distinguish this plant, which forms a dense clump offering textural interest. Not a true fern, but rather a member of the asparagus genus.

Ginger (*Alpinia* spp., *Costus* spp., *Curcuma* spp., *Globba* spp., *Hedychium* spp., *Kaempferia* spp., and *Zingiber* spp.)
Zones 8–10. Height: 1–10'. Peacock gingers (*Kaempferia pulchra*, *Kaempferia masoniana*, *Kaempferia robusta*, and *Kaempferia grande*) are wonderful for ground cover in shaded locations and have low-growing, variegated leaves and springtime white and purple blooms. Heat and humidity are necessary for good bloom and leaf production. Moist but well-drained, organic soils preferred. Shell ginger (*Alpinia zerumbet*) can grow to ten feet, and like many of the gingers can be invasive in some areas, spreading by underground rhizomes. Cold tolerance depends on variety.

Golden plume (*Schaueria flavicoma*)
Zones 8–11. Height: 2'. Handsome plumes of bright yellow light up shady beds from the spring through summer months. Somewhat cold tolerant, and very tolerant of heat and humidity.

Hardy orchid (*Calanthe* spp.)
Zones 8–10. Height: 1–2'. Variety of blooming terrestrial orchid. 'Kozu Spice' is spring-blooming and has white-and-red, yellow-and-red, or pink-and-red blossoms on twelve-inch stalks above evergreen, pleated leaves. *Calanathe reflexa* is summer-blooming with two-tone pink-and-white flowers on twelve-inch stalks. Narrow, pleated evergreen leaves form a fifteen-inch rosette. *Calanthe sieboldii* is spring-blooming, with pansy-like flowers in white, gold, red, and brown on fifteen-inch stalks. Evergreen, deeply pleated foliage forms fifteen-inch-wide rosettes. All prefer partial sun to shade.

Holly fern (*Cyrtomium falcatum*)
Zones 8–11. Height: 2'. A handsome and hardy evergreen fern with leathery foliage that forms compact clumps. Somewhat drought tolerant once established, but requires a shaded location and ample moisture.

Impatiens (*Impatiens walleriana*)
Zones 10–11. Height: 1–2'. (See Annuals—Shade section entry.)

Jewels of Opar (*Talinum paniculatum*)
Zones 9–10. Height: 24–30". (See Annuals—Sun section entry.)

Leatherleaf fern (*Rumohra adiantiformis*)
Zones 8–11. Height: 1–3'. Excellent evergreen ground cover with leathery, dark-green fronds that form thick clumps, this fern prefers well-drained, rich organic soils. This is the familiar fern used by florists.

Leopard plant (*Farfugium japonicum*)
Zones 8–10. Height: 1–3'. Large, umbrella-like leaves speckled with yellow and yellow, daisy-like blooms. Shade and rich organic soils preferred.

Lycoris or hurricane lily (*Lycoris* spp.)
Zones 8–9. Height: 2'. (See Perennials—Sun section entry.)

Malaysian orchid (*Medinilla myriantha*)
Zones 9B–10. Height: 4'. Handsome plant with large ovate leaves and clusters of small pink bracts. Prefers bright shade, adequate moisture, and a rich organic soil. (See Plate 27.)

Mondo grass (*Ophiopogon japonicus*)
Zones 8–10. Height: 6–12". (See Perennials—Sun section entry.)

Monkey grass or lily turf (*Liriope muscari*)
Zones 8–11. Height: 6–10". Grass-like ground cover that forms clumps and spreads slowly. Lilac-lavender flower spikes. 'Peedee Ingot' hybrid has chartreuse-golden foliage and hybrid 'Okina,' also known as frosted monkey grass, has foliage that is tipped and speckled with white.

Mouse ear hawkweed (*Pilosella officinarum*)
Zones 8–10. Height: 2". Surface-spreading ground cover with felt-textured, silver-gray foliage that makes small rosettes which spread by aboveground stolons. In early summer, the mats are topped with one-inch, light-yellow flowers on eight-inch-tall stalks. Tolerant of heat and humidity. Grow in partial shade to provide dramatic accents around the base of other plants.

Nun's orchid (*Phaius tankervillae*)
Zones 9–11. Height: 3–5'. Terrestrial orchid with evergreen, paddle-shaped, pleated leaves that forms a thick clump of showy springtime spikes covered in three-inch blooms in colors from lavender to white to yellows. Rich organic soils and filtered sun preferred. Needs freeze protection in colder areas. (See Plate 28.)

Oxblood lily (*Rhodophiala bifida*)
Zones 8–10. Height: 1'. Amaryllis relative that multiplies steadily. Lycoris-like bulbs with evergreen foliage that goes dormant in late spring. Beginning in late summer or early fall, one-foot stalks form and are topped with a cluster of carmine-red flowers. Pink oxblood lily (*Rhodophiala bifida*, variant *spathacea*) is pink-flowered with small, bright, magenta flowers atop eight-inch stems in August or September. After flowering, the lycoris-like basal foliage emerges and persists through winter. Grow in rich soil in partial sun to light shade.

Peacock ginger (*Kaempferia* spp.)
Zones 8–11. Height: 6–12". Intricately patterned, large leaves and small white or lavender blooms in summer make this ginger a good choice for ground cover in shaded beds. Depending on variety, leaf colors range from green/silver to green/burgundy.

Persian shield (*Strobilanthes* spp.)
Zones 9–11. Height: 3'. (See Annuals—Shade section entry.)

Peruvian lily (*Alstroemeria* spp.)
Zones 8–10. Height: 1–2'. While the red-blooming species of the genus *Alstroemeria* can be aggressive, hybrids are more manageable and come in a range of bloom colors, some of which are present from spring to late summer. Makes a good cut flower with two-inch, lily-like blooms. (See Plate 29.)

Platt's black (*Leptinella squalida*)
Zones 8–10. Height: 2". Low-growing, feathery, fern-like foliage hugs the ground. 'Brass Buttons' variety has attractive green-and-bronze foliage. Grow in partial shade.

Polka-dot plant (*Hypoestes phyllostachya*)
Zones 8–11. Height: 1'. Colorful, pale- to deep-pink polka- dotted plant that is often used as a ground cover or massed for effect. Does best in partial shade and is somewhat drought tolerant. Needs cold protection. Plants will reseed and can be rooted from cuttings.

Red flame ivy or 'Dragon's Breath' or waffle plant (*Hemigraphis* spp.)
Zones 9–11. Height: 6–12". Colorful foliage on a low-growing plant, with many varieties available. Root cuttings for more plants.

Sacred lily (*Rohdea japonica*)
Zones 8–10. Height: 1'. Has the appearance of an evergreen hosta with strap-like, thick, dark-green leaves forming an upright, cylindrical clump about two feet wide. Insignificant flowers produce short stalks of red berries at the base of the plant. When used in mass, hybrids such as 'Chirimen Boshi,' 'Talbot Manor,' or 'Gunjaku' offer variegated foliage. Provide partial to full shade.

Sanchezia (*Sanchezia nobilis*)
Zones 9–11. Height: 1–8'. Upright growth and dark-green, waxy leaves that are deeply veined with yellow provide color and accent in shade beds. May need frequent pruning to maintain shape. Needs cold protection. Very tolerant of heat and humidity.

Stromanthe, 'Triostar' variety (*Stromanthe sanguinea*)
Zones 9B–11. Height 1–2'. Dramatic plant with tricolor foliage that prefers filtered shade and can be grown in a container. Large, paddle-shaped, variegated green-and-white leaves with deep-pink/purple undersides. Provide rich soil and adequate moisture. Its small blooms resemble those of birds-of-paradise. (See Plate 30.)

Tongue fern (*Pyrrosia lingua*)
Zones 8–10. Height: 10–12". The fern's rhizome grows along the ground, sending out cardboard-textured leaves with a felt-like backside. Makes a nice evergreen mass. A variegated tongue fern, 'Ogon Nishiki' (*Pyrrosia lingua*), forms a dense colony two feet wide with thick, green, vertically held leaves with diagonal, butterscotch-yellow banding. 'Five-Fingered' tongue fern (*Pyrrosia polydactyla*) makes a foot-wide clump of felt-like, five-fingered dark-green leaves. All types prefer partial sun to light shade.

Trailing wishbone flower (*Torenia fournieri*)
Zones 10–11. Height: 3–6". (See Annuals—Sun section entry.)

Yellow shrimp plant or lollipop plant (*Pachystachys lutea*)
Zones 9–11. Height: 3–5'. Showy bloom spikes of yellow with white from spring through fall above upright green foliage. Prune heavily to maintain it and encourage flowering. Needs cold protection in northern portions of the state.

Vines

Allamanda (*Mandevilla* spp.)
Zones 9–11. Length: 20'. Large, trumpet-like blooms in pink or yellow on this evergreen vine. Blooms much of the year in southern portions of the state, and may need cold protection farther north.

Bougainvillea (*Bougainvillea* spp.)
Zones 9–11. Length: 2–10'. Long, thorny canes which produce brightly colored, showy bracts in winter through late spring. Very heat and drought tolerant, this vine prefers well-drained soils and full sun.

Bower vine (*Pandorea jasminoides*)
Zones 9–11. Length: 15'+. A tropical vine for northern as well as southern zones of Florida with glossy, dark-green foliage and clusters of attractive, funnel-shaped flowers in white with crimson throats or, in the case of the 'Rosea' variety, pale-pink blooms accented with crimson. 'Lady Di' is white with a creamy white throat, and 'Alba' is all white. Grow in full sun with rich organic soil and regular moisture.

Chalice vine (*Solandra maxima*)
Zones 10–11. Length: 10'+. Large, golden, trumpet-shaped blooms with night-time fragrance on vigorous vines that require substantial support. Partial shade preferred.

Clematis (*Clematis* spp.)
Zones 8–11. Length: 2–8'. This genus includes a number of vining plants that climb by clasping and produce showy flowers in a range of deep, velvety colors in spring. Best grown where their root area can be shaded by other plants and where afternoon shade is present. Well-drained, rich organic soils are preferred. Do not let roots dry out. The native *Clematis crispa* species produces one- to two-inch white bell-shaped flowers with recurved petals showing purple underneath. Recommended are: *Clematis armandii*, 'Snowdrift' and 'Appleblossom,' *Clematis reticulata*, *Clematis viticella*, and *Clematis texensis*. 'Rooguchi' and 'Niobe' also recommended. (See Plate 2.)

Combretum (*Combretum grandiflorum*)
Zone 11. Length: 20'+. Slender climbing vine with clusters of showy red blooms followed by clumps of papery winged fruits. Full sun is preferable for best flowering.

False hydrangea vine (*Schizophragma* spp.)
Zones 8–9. Length: 50'. Hybrid 'Moonlight' has pewter-blue leaves veined with green and pink and big white flowers; 'Roseum' has pink blooms in summer followed by dark-red petioles; 'Strawberry Leaf' has strawberry-like leaves and white, teardrop sepals in summer. Partial shade preferred, as is substantial support, such as a large tree.

Flame vine (*Pyrostegia venusta*)
Zones 9–11. Length: 15'+. Lush tropical color in an evergreen, woody vine that blooms in late winter with large clusters of four-inch-long, brilliantly orange, tubular flowers. Good for fences, but restrict from trees, where it can grow uncontrollably. Prune hard after it blooms. Salt tolerant. (See Plate 14.)

Mandevilla (*Mandevilla sanderi* and *Mandevilla splendens*)
Zones 9–11. Length: 20'. Showy, trumpet-like blooms. Good container specimen. Will need cold protection in northern zones.

Philodendron (*Philodendron giganteum*)
Zones 9–11. Length: 40'+. Planted where it will climb the trunk of a large tree, this vine's leaves will increase in size as it grows higher, some to more than a foot wide. Most of the nearly four hundred species of philodendron prefer shade, rich soil, and tropical conditions, though well-established examples have grown back from the roots in Zone 9 after experiencing freezing temperatures.

Pride of the Cape (*Bauhinia* spp.)
Zones 10–11. Length: 10'. Sprawling shrub or evergreen flowering vine produces red blooms in summer followed by five-inch, dark-brown seedpods. Pruning keeps the plant in bounds.

Philodendron (*Philodendron giganteum*) adds a touch of the tropics with its big, colorful foliage. This individual is thriving in a northeastern Florida garden.

Purple-painted trumpet vine (*Clytostoma callistegioides*)
Zones 8–11. Length: 10–20'. A highly recommended flowering vine for partially shaded locations everywhere in the state, but especially good for northern growers who cannot keep tropical vines. Produces showy, three-inch, purple, trumpet-shaped blooms in spring. Evergreen foliage is a dark, leathery green.

Queen's wreath (*Petrea volubilis*)
Zones 10–11. Length: 20'. Evergreen vine with rough leaves and showy clusters of small purple or white blooms in the spring and early summer that resemble wisteria. Full sun to partial shade.

Rex begonia vine (*Cissus discolor*)
Zones 9–11. Length: 1–10'. Slender vine that thrives on heat and humidity. Oblong, pointed leaves display deeply veined colors of green, silver, pink, and dark red. Partial to full shade. May need cold protection in Zone 9.

Sky flower or clock vine or sky vine (*Thunbergia grandiflora*)
Zones 9–11. Length: 10'. Attractive, large, trumpet-shaped flowers up to four inches across in white to pale- or deep-blue to purple depending on variety. Blooms from spring through fall. Has evergreen foliage and can grow aggressively in southern portions of the state. May need cold protection in Zone 9.

Blue sky flower or skyflower (*Thunbergia grandiflora*) delivers almost nonstop blooms but will need cold protection in northern Florida.

Sweet potato, 'Blackie,' 'Margarita,' and tricolor varieties (*Ipomoea batatas*)
Zones 8–11. Length: 4'. Low-growing, creeping, colorful foliage in chartreuse, variegated, or nearly black extends from these tuber vegetables. Best confined to container plantings as they can spread rapidly by forming new tubers. Full sun to light
shade is preferred. Newer varieties offer more compact growth habits.

Swiss cheese plant (*Monstera friedrichstahlii*)
Zones 10–11. Length: 10'+. Foot-long leaves with multiple holes distinguish this
vine, which is best grown in a shaded, moist location with a tree or other strong
support. Its common name, Swiss cheese plant, is also often applied to *Monstera
deliciosa*.

Shrubs

Abelia (*Abelia schumannii*)
Zones 8–9. Height: 3–6'. 'Bumblebee' is just one of several flowering abelias, offering two- to three-inch-long lavender, foxglove-like blooms early in spring. Others
include 'Golden Anniversary,' with white blooms, 'Confetti,' with pink, white, and
green foliage, and 'Edward Goucher,' with lavender-purple blooms.

Azaleas (*Rhododendron* spp.)
Zones 8–10. Height: 2–6'. Native varieties (Florida azalea *Rhododendron austrinum*
and *Rhododendron canescens*) as well as the Indian and Kurume azaleas are popular
evergreen landscape shrubs in a range of sizes from mini-plants to large mounded
shrubs. All bloom in early spring with trumpet-shaped blooms in oranges, yellows, pinks, whites, and deep rose. Shallow-rooted, these acid-loving plants do
well in well-drained, acidic soils that receive adequate moisture and midday shade.
Drought tolerant once established. The 'Encore' series offers repeat blooms over
three seasons.

Bluebeard (*Caryopteris x clandonensis* and *Caryopteris incana*)
Zones 8–9. Height: 5'. 'Petit Bleu' variety offers a compact growth pattern and in-
tense drifts of deep-blue blooms complemented by glossy green foliage. 'Sunshine
Blue' has variegated, sunny, yellow-and-green foliage that sets off its pale-blue
blooms. 'Pink Chablis' has nonstop pink blooms from summer through autumn.
All attract butterflies.

Butterfly bush (*Buddleia asiatica*, *B. madagascariensis*)
Zones 8–11. Height: 4–6'. Fountain-like growth with silvery foliage and buttery-
yellow to white blooms from spring through fall. (See Plate 31.) Roots well from cuttings. 'Lo & Behold' series 'Blue Chip' has ever-present blue flowers and a compact,
mounded growth habit that reaches to twenty inches. Suitable in Zone 9 and up.

Camellia (*Camellia* spp.)
Zones 8–9. Height: 5–40'. Handsome evergreen flowering shrubs with waxy, deep-

green foliage and showy midwinter blooms that vary from reds to pinks to white with variegations depending on hybrid. *Camellia japonica* blooms early in spring and *Camellia sasanqua* blooms later. Partial shade and slightly acidic, rich soils recommended for best flowering. *Camellia sinensis* (suitable for Zones 8–9) is the plant that produces tea.

Crape myrtle (*Lagerstroemia indica*)
Zones 8–10. Height: 3–20'. Very showy clusters of frilled blooms in a wide range of colors from white to red in spring through summer on this deciduous shrub with attractive bark and an upright growth habit. Dwarf cultivars offer improved blooms and disease resistance in a smaller package. 'Razzle Dazzle' dwarf crape myrtles come in a variety of colors from white through deep red and have bloom times from late summer through fall. Drought tolerant once established. Full sun is preferred.

Croton (*Codiaeum variegatum*)
Zones 9–11. Height: 5–10'. Variously colored and patterned leaves adorn this evergreen shrub. Leaf shapes vary from large, paddle-like shapes to narrow "fingers." Needs cold protection in northern portions of state. Easily rooted from cuttings. (See Plate 12.)

Cycad (*Cycad* spp., *Zamia* spp., and *Dioon* spp.)
Zones 8–11. Height: 3–20'. An ancient variety of plants, many have leathery, palm-like fronds and palm-like growth habits. Recommended cycads include: cardboard palm (*Zamia furfuracea*), coontie (*Zamia floridana*), and queen sago (*Ceratozamia mexicana*).

Florida anise (*Illicium floridanum*)
Zones 8–10. Height: 5–20'. (See Native Plants section entry.)

Florida boxwood (*Schaefferia frutescens*)
Zones 10–11. Height: 2–5' (See Native Plants section entry.)

Forest bell bush (*Mackaya bella*)
Zones 9–11. Height: 6'. Evergreen shrub with spring blooms of purple-veined, white, bell-shaped flowers. Bright, filtered shade and moist conditions preferred.

Gallberry (*Ilex glabra*)
Zones 8–11. Height: 10'. (See Native Plants section entry.)

Gardenia (*Gardenia jasminoides*)
Zones 9–11. Height: 3–8'. Evergreen shrub with dense, glossy foliage and showy, fragrant early summer blossoms. Shade and well-drained, slightly acidic soils preferred. Plants with varying bloom forms are available, as are dwarf varieties, including 'Heaven Scent,' which prefers more sun than do most gardenias.

Golden dewdrop (*Duranta erecta*)
Zones 8–11. Height: 4–6'. (See Native Plants section entry.)

Grape holly (*Mahonia* spp.)
Zones 8–11. Height: 6–12'. Handsome, spiny evergreen foliage and upright growth habit. Best suited to partially shaded locations.

Hibiscus (*Hibiscus rosa-sinensis*)
Zones 9–11. Height: 4–10'. Glossy green or variegated foliage with a mounded growth habit and a long bloom period of large (up to a foot wide), colorful flowers with single, double, and ruffled petals. Some hibiscuses are trained as standard plants and make wonderful container specimens. May need cold protection in some areas. Good salt tolerance.

Honey flower (*Melianthus major*)
Zones 8–10. Height: 3–10'. Giant honey flower is grown for its attractive, finely toothed leaves. A large shrub to small tree, it grows best in full sun with moist but well-drained, rich soil. Prune hard in spring for a fresh crop of leaves.

Hydrangea (*Hydrangea macrophylla*)
Zones 8–9. Height: 5'. Bigleaf hydrangeas are best suited to northern portions of

Oakleaf hydrangea (*Hydrangea quercifolia*) is a native hydrangea with prodigious blooms.

the state, with compact growth habits and large, showy heads of blooms in whites, blues, pinks, and reds, some of which are double. Newer varieties from the 'Endless Summer' and 'Forever & Ever' series bloom on both new and old wood. Compact hybrids such as 'Midnight Dutchess,' 'Queen of Pearls,' 'Princess Lace,' and 'Mini Penny' offer big blooms on smaller plants that are suitable for container culture as well as inground applications.

Ixora (*Ixora* spp.)
Zones 10–11. Height: 15'. Showy, large heads of yellow to red blooms and a very compact growth habit distinguish this popular shrub. Somewhat salt tolerant. Grow in full sun.

Jatropha (*Jatropha* spp.)
Zones 10–11. Height: 4–15'. Shrubs or small trees with almost constantly spectacular flowers and dramatic foliage.

Lady palm (*Rhapis excelsa*)
Zones 8–11. Height: 3–10'. Clump-forming evergreen dwarf palm with bright-green fronds. Grow in shade with adequate moisture. Excellent container specimen. *Rhapis Akatsuki* is a variegated cultivar.

Loropetalum or Chinese fringe bush (*Loropetalum chinense*)
Zones 8–10. Height: 3–8'. Attractive, fine, evergreen foliage often burgundy in color. Abundant spring bloom of tiny purple to red flowers. Excellent choice for all-season color and interest. A good hedge plant and choice shrub, or train as a standard. Full sun to partial shade and well-drained soil preferred. 'Ever Red' has burgundy foliage and prolific deep-red blooms. 'Little Rose Dawn' has profuse deep-pink, frilly blooms. 'Carolina Moonlight' is a compact shrub with large, profuse white blooms. Other low-maintenance examples are 'Purple Diamond,' which has showy, pink, springtime blooms and rich purple foliage, and 'Purple Pixie,' a diminutive one- to two-foot-tall shrub with similar flowers and foliage. Suitable for containers too. (See Plate 13.)

Monstera or Swiss cheese plant (*Monstera deliciosa*)
Zones 9–11. Height: 3–6'. Lush tropical look with very large evergreen leaves and edible fruit in late summer. Can be aggressive in southern locations. Leathery, brown leaf sheaths are often dried for craft use.

Natal plum (*Carissa macrocarpa*)
Zones 10–11. Height: 10'. Glossy, dark-green evergreen shrub with fragrant, white, two-inch blooms that produce two-inch edible fruits year-round. Very heat and salt tolerant. Dwarf cultivars include 'Boxwood Beauty,' 'Linki,' and 'Dainty Princess.'

Needle palm (*Rhapidophyllum hystrix*)
Zones 8–11. Height: 8'. (See Native Plants section entry.)

Pheasant berry (*Leycesteria formosa*)
Zones 8–10. Height: 3–5'. Recommended hybrid 'Golden Lanterns' has a rounded form with chartreuse foliage tipped with red, four-inch, pendulous clusters of purple-red bracts with white flowers in summer, followed by edible, dark-purple berries—these fruits have been reported to taste like caramel or chocolate.

Pomegranate (*Punica granatum*)
Zones 8–11. Height: 5–20'. Large bush or small tree with deciduous, fine foliage and showy orange blooms in spring; summer brings round fruits with thick skins and edible, juicy seeds. 'State Fair' variety is a dwarf suitable for container culture and yields many flowers and small fruits. Plant in full sun for best performance.

Quince (*Chaenomeles* spp.)
Zones 8–9. Height: 3–6'. Striking early spring blooms in pink to orange to red on a variety of hybrids of Japanese and standard quince. 'Crimson and Gold' (*Chaenomeles x superba*) has large, velvety, crimson blooms and a low-spreading growth habit. 'Kingishi' offers a medium growth pattern and large, showy, single orange blooms.

Rose (*Rosa* spp.)
Zones 8–11. Height: 2–6'. Heirloom roses are a wide variety of bushy plants with showy single or double blooms that are often quite fragrant. Heirloom roses are not grafted and new plants can be rooted from cuttings. Recommended varieties include 'Louis Philippe,' 'Mrs. R. B. Cant,' and 'Zephirine Drouhin.' (See Plate 2.)

Rose, hybrid (*Rosa* spp.)
Zones 8–11. Height: 1–5'. Recommended are 'Knockout,' 'Easy Elegance,' and 'Oso Easy,' which yield a wide range of bloom colors. Hybrid plants are resistant to black spot and mildew. Most are low-growing, with some providing good ground cover, and have single- or double-petal blooms.

Saw palmetto (*Serenoa repens*)
Zones 8–11. Height: 6'. (See Native Plants section entry.)

Silver buttonwood (*Conocarpus erectus* variety *sericeus*)
Zones 10–11. Height: 4–20'. (See Native Plants section entry.)

Summersweet (*Clethra alnifolia*)
Zones 8–9. Height: 2–5'. Fragrant spikes of summer flowers and an upright growth habit. 'Ruby Spice' variety has fragrant, reddish-pink flowers and yellow fall color. 'Hummingbird' cultivar has dark-green foliage and fragrant white flower spikes. Best grown in moist, shaded locations.

Sweetshrub (*Calycanthus floridus*)
Zones 8–9. Height: 6–10'. (See Native Plants section entry.)

Texas sage (*Leucophyllum frutescens*)
Zones 8–11. Height: 8'. Low, spreading growth habit, finely textured, silvery, evergreen foliage, and small purple blossoms from spring through summer. Drought tolerant.

Virginia willow or sweetspire (*Itea virginica*)
Zones 8–9. Height: 3'. (See Native Plants section entry.)

Yaupon holly (*Ilex vomitoria*)
Zones 8–10. Height: 1–10'. (See Native Plants section entry.)

Small and Dwarf Trees

Bamboo palm (*Chamaedorea seifrizii*)
Zones 9–11. Height: 8–12'. Small clustering palm that prefers bright filtered sun. Attractive, broad leaves and bamboo-like segmented trunks.

Bellflower (*Portulandia grandiflora*)
Zones 10–11. Height: 6–10'. Evergreen small tree or shrub native to Jamaica and the Virgin Islands. Large, fragrant, white, funnel-shaped flowers in warmer months atop glossy, dark-green foliage. Prefers light shade and regular moisture in summer and drier conditions in winter.

Bismarck palm (*Bismarckia nobilis*)
Zones 9–11. Height: 10'+. Sculptured shape and dramatic, stiff, silvery fronds. Good heat, salt, and drought tolerance. Full sun preferred.

Cat palm (*Chamaedorea cataractarum*)
Zones 10B–11. Height: 5'. Fronds appear from the base of this small palm, forming a clump of dark-green foliage. Good for containers or landscape uses in partial sun to partial shade with adequate moisture.

Chamaedorea palm (*Chamaedorea* spp.)
Zone 11. Height: 10'. Dwarf palm with an upright growth habit. Requires a shaded location for good performance.

Chastetree (*Vitex* spp.)
Zones 8–9. Height: 4–10'. Hybrid 'Abbeville Blue' has fragrant, foot-long spikes of clear-blue blooms throughout the summer, while 'Shoal Creek' has fragrant, deep-blue flower heads throughout summer. Both are recommended. Good cut flowers. 'Alba' variety has variegated foliage and white blooms.

Cockspur coral tree (*Erythrina crista-galli*)
Zones 9–11. Height: 25'. Brilliant red blooms in late summer and early fall are followed by long, brown seedpods on this shrubby small tree.

Cocoplum (*Chrysobalanus icaco*)
Zones 10–11. Height: 10–20'. (See Native Plants section entry.)

Dahoon (*Ilex cassine*)
Zones 8–11. Height: 40'. (See Native Plants section entry.)

Dogwood (*Cornus florida*)
Zones 8–9. Height: 15–40'. (See Native Plants section entry.)

Dwarf banana (*Musa acuminata*)
Zones 8–11. Height: 6'. Big, tropical, paddle-shaped leaves. Recommended varieties include 'Dwarf Cavendish' and 'Super Dwarf Cavendish.' Good for container plantings as bananas tend to form dense clumps. May die back after freezing temperatures but often recovers.

Dwarf citrus types, such as calamondin, kumquat, Kaffir lime, and 'Meyer Improved' lemon (*Citrus* spp.)
Zones 9–11. Height: 4–6'. Smaller varieties and dwarf cultivars make excellent container specimens in northern zones where they can be moved indoors during freezes. When planted in the ground, many can reach heights of ten feet or more. Grow in full sun in rich, well-drained soil with adequate moisture. Fragrant early spring blooms, followed by edible fruits.

European fan palm (*Chamaerops humilis*)
Zones 8–11. Height: 15'. Clump-forming dwarf palm with palmate, gray-green foliage.

Fiddlewood (*Citharexylum fruticosum*)
Zone 11. Height: 25'. (See Native Plants section entry.)

Fishtail palm (*Caryota mitis*)
Zones 9B–11. Height: 10–25'. Flashy foliage with "fish-tail" fronds. Grow in partial sun to full shade and provide adequate moisture and good drainage. The fishtail palm is a shallow-rooted plant that forms large clumps, and it is useful in combination plantings in shady areas. Several attractive cultivars are available. Wind protection is suggested. Fishtail palm will tolerate light frosts. Divide clumps and separate suckers from the parent clump for more plants. Good container specimen, and can be grown indoors.

Florida thatch palm or Caribbean thatch palm (*Thrinax radiata*)
Zones 10–11. Height: 15'. (See Native Plants section entry.)

Florida yew (*Taxus floridana*)
Zones 8–9. Height: 20'. (See Native Plants section entry.)

Frangipani (*Plumeria* spp.)
Zones 10–11. Height: 12'. Thick, rubbery trunks and limbs with large leaves, Frangipani are grown for their attractive and fragrant blooms. They are often deciduous in winter, though evergreen varieties are available. Salt tolerant. Full sun to partial shade preferred.

Geiger tree (*Cordia sebestena*)
Zones 10–11. Height: 10–30'. (See Native Plants section entry.)

Hawthorn (*Crataegus* spp.)
Zones 8–10. Height: 25'. (See Native Plants section entry.)

Jamaican silver thatch palm (*Coccothrinax jamaicensis*)
Zones 10–11. Height: 5–10'. A miniature palm with attractive fronds which can be used in coil-method and woven basket-making. Prefers well-drained, alkaline soils and can tolerate some shade.

Jatropha (*Jatropha* spp.)
Zones 10–11. Height: 4–15'. Shrubs or small trees with almost constant spectacular flowers and dramatic foliage.

Kumquat (*Fortunella* spp.)
Zones 8–11. Height: 15'. Grown for their edible, orange fruit. Dense foliage and a compact growth habit. Full sun preferred.

Lignum vitae (*Guaiacum sanctum*)
Zones 10–11. Height: 10–30'. (See Native Plants section entry.)

Lipstick palm or sealing wax palm (*Cyrtostachys renda*)
Zone 11. Height:10–30'. Dramatic, glossy red crown-shafts. Very slow-growing palm that prefers filtered sun and moist, fertile soils. Very cold sensitive and recommended only for the southernmost regions of the state. Has a striking appearance that makes its difficulty to grow worthwhile.

Lipstick tree (*Bixa orellana*)
Zones 10–11. Height: 10–20'. Compact evergreen tree that provides winter color with clusters of pale-lavender blooms followed by bristly, crimson fruits. Grow in full sun.

Loquat (*Eriobotrya japonica*)
Zones 9–11. Height: 20'. Attractive specimen tree with large, leathery, evergreen foliage, a spring bloom period, and small, edible fruits that taste like a combination of a peach and an apricot. Compact growth habit. Plant in full sun for best performance. Somewhat salt tolerant.

Old man palm (*Coccothrinax crinita*) is a very slow-growing tree with a distinctively hairy trunk that makes it an excellent specimen for South Florida gardens.

Madagascar palm (*Chrysalidocarpus lutescens*)
Zones 10–11. Height: 30'. Graceful, feathery fronds and attractive, bamboo-like trunks that often grow in clumps. Prefers partial to full shade and fertile, acidic soil.

Old man palm (*Coccothrinax crinita*)
Zones 10–11. Height: 15'. Extremely slow-growing palm with a distinctive, decorative, fibrous trunk. Good specimen tree.

Palmetto (*Sabal minor*)
Zones 8–11. Height: 4'. (See Native Plants section entry.)

Papaya (*Carica papaya*)
Zones 9–11. Height: 15'. Succulent evergreen shrub or small tree that produces a mass of large, showy, lobed leaves and edible fruits.

Pawpaw (*Asimina obovata*)
Zones 8–10. Height: 5–30'. (See Native Plants section entry.)

Purple jacaranda (*Jacaranda jasminoides*)
Zones 10–11. Height: 15'. Small evergreen tree or large shrub that blooms throughout the year with large clusters of trumpet-shaped, deep-purple flowers. Grow in full sun to partial shade in well-drained, rich, organic soil.

Pygmy date palm (*Phoenix roebelenii*)
Zones 10–11. Height: 8'. Delicate foliage forming a miniature, full-scale crown atop a straight or curved trunk.

Red buckeye (*Aesculus pavia*)
Zones 8–9. Height: 6–25'. (See Native Plants section entry.)

Rhodoleia (*Rhodoleia championii*)
Zones 8–9. Height: 15'. Evergreen foliage and an open growth pattern with showy clusters of deep-pink blooms in winter. Tolerates partial shade.

Ruffled fan palm or licuala palm (*Licuala grandis*)
Zones 10–11. Height: 10'. Large, fused-leaf fronds. Best in filtered sun. Another cultivar, the ornamental *Licuala peltata* subspecies *sumawongii*, has four- to five-foot-wide fused fronds with pinked margins.

Sea grape (*Coccoloba uvifera*)
Zones 9–11. Height: 3–35'. (See Native Plants section entry.)

Seven-son flower (*Heptacodium miconioides*)
Zones 8–9. Height: 10'. Glossy, arching, dark-green foliage, textural, exfoliating bark, and fragrant, creamy, late-summer blooms followed by clusters of striking reddish-pink sepals in fall.

Silver palm (*Coccothrinax argentata*)
Zones 10–11. Height: 5–20'. (See Native Plants section entry.)

Simpson's stopper (*Myrcianthes fragrans*)
Zones 8–11. Height: 25'. (See Native Plants section entry.)

Spicewood (*Calyptranthes pallens*)
Zones 10–11. Height: 20'. (See Native Plants section entry.)

Ti (*Cordyline* spp.)
Zones 10–11. Height: 8'. Forming a colorful shrub or small tree, the ti has showy variegated foliage in colors from greens to rich purples. Grow in partial shade with rich, organic soil. May need cold protection and can be grown in a container.

1. Punch up your landscape's color impact with a brilliant planter or pot to contrast or coordinate with various flower and foliage hues. Elevating a pot such as this increases visibility and adds height.

2. A 'Zephirine Drouhin' heirloom rose and a 'Rooguchi' clematis make good garden partners.

3. Agapanthus (*Agapanthus* spp.) is a perennial favorite in Florida gardens, with blooms available in a range of blues and whites.

4. Contrasting colors pop when paired in the garden or planters.

5. The brilliant colors of a large bromeliad and a purple heart (*Tradescantia pallida*) ground cover virtually bounce off each other in this little landscape at Fairchild Tropical Botanic Garden in Coral Gables, Florida. Massing like colors increases impact, as does pairing opposites on the color wheel.

6. Replace turf with a ground cover such as this melampodium and kiss mowing goodbye.

7. Anole lizards eat large volumes of insects, making them indispensable garden allies. Wildlife enhances the gardening experience in many ways.

8. Water gardens can pack a wallop of color with plants such as this aquatic iris.

9. Who says fruit trees can't be ornamental too? This variegated lemon produces pink-fleshed fruits with striped skins.

10. Pick Japanese persimmons as they ripen on the tree.

11. A troupe of leggy insects visits arrowhead blooms growing in a tiny water garden.

12. The familiar croton is a good choice for year-round color because of its colorful and varied foliage. In northern areas, gardeners will need to provide cold protection for this colorful shrub.

13. Loropetalum (*Loropetalum* spp.) blooms in early spring.

14. Flame vine (*Pyrostegia venusta*) provides brilliant winter blooms for South Florida gardens.

15. French mallow (*Malva sylvestris*) is an heirloom flowering annual that can be grown from seed.

16. A lush landscape such as this one requires little of the gardener but provides plenty of shade, texture, color, and wildlife habitat.

17. A brick path leads the visitor through this area of the Key West Garden Club's Martello Tower Gardens.

18. Even a hostile seaside environment with high wind and salt spray can be enhanced with easily maintained plantings of sea grapes, agaves, and melampodium.

19. Planters in long-term storage are surrounded by landscape cloth to suppress weeds.

20. This front-step arrangement takes potted plantings off ground level. Notice that one of the pots is set upon an inverted pot to add further height.

21. Before planting, place shrubs, perennials, and annuals while still in their pots to help determine their eventual location in the bed. It's a lot easier to move them around before planting.

22. Save your back by using a hand truck to move heavy pots, rocks, and bags of fertilizer or soil.

23. Young gardeners will enjoy observing and learning about the many insects found in the garden.

24. Jacobinia (*Justicia carnea*) adds a punch of color to any planting scheme.

25. Coleus (*Solenostemon scutellarioides*) can be fashioned into an attractive topiary given time and patience.

26. Lion's tail (*Leonoitis nepetifolia*) can be grown from seed and may become a perennial under favorable conditions. These tall plants (three to five feet) have striking orange blooms.

27. The Malaysian orchid (*Medinilla myrianta*) is not actually an orchid species, but it still makes a dramatic addition to any garden.

28. The nun's orchid (*Phaius tankervillae*) is a terrestrial orchid with attractive foliage and handsome spikes of early spring blooms.

29. The Peruvian lily (*Alstromeria* spp.) provides lovely blooms, making it a great choice for lightly shaded gardens.

30. The tropical foliage of Stromanthe (*Stromanthe sanguinea*) provides year-round color. In northern portions of the state it will need cold protection.

31. Butterfly bush (*Buddleia madagascariensis*) is a reliable choice for Florida gardens and produces silvery-green foliage with butter-yellow blooms.

32. Native *Clematis crispa* produces a flurry of inch-long, bell-shaped flowers in late spring and early summer. This perennial vine can be trained to a trellis or a fence.

Tree fern (*Cyathea* spp.)
Zones 9–11. Height: 20'. Ancient genus of ferns that form dramatic small trees with distinct trunks and frond foliage. Various cultivars are available. May need cold protection in northern zones and are best planted in rich, organic soils with full to partial shade.

Uncarina (*Uncarina grandidieri*)
Zones 9–11. Height: 10'. Small tree with large, showy yellow, trumpet-shaped blooms (*Uncarina abbreviata* has pink/violet blooms) during warmer months. Prefers full sun and well-drained, alkaline, sandy soil. Good drought tolerance.

Wax myrtle (*Myrica cerifera*)
Zones 8–11. Height: 25'. (See Native Plants section entry.)

Wild cinnamon (*Canella winterana*)
Zone 11. Height: 15–25'. (See Native Plants section entry.)

Windmill palm (*Trachycarpus fortunei*)
Zones 8–11. Height: 20'. Cold-tolerant palm with an upright form.

Window palm (*Reinhardtia latisecta*)
Zones 10–11. Height: 10'. A dainty palm with fused fronds that is best for shaded locations with rich, well-drained soils.

Yellow bells, yellow elder or esperanza (*Tecoma stans*)
Zones 10–11. Height: 15'. Evergreen shrub or tree with clusters of yellow or orange bell- shaped blooms throughout the summer in northern Florida and year-round elsewhere. Very tolerant of heat and humidity. A tropical plant, it requires cold protection. Grow in full sun for best blooms.

Zombie palm (*Zombia antillarum*)
Zones 10–11. Height: 15'. Clumping palm best grown in full sun. Displays a very textural trunk with an attractive spiral pattern.

Native Plants

Perennials

Bartram's ixia (*Calydorea caelestina*)
Zones 8–10. Height: 6". Grow this rare and threatened plant, originally found only in a small area in northeastern Florida, in full to partial sun. Its six-inch-long, green-pleated, iris-like leaves form a small clump. Starting in early summer and

continuing into late summer, these clumps will be topped with six-inch stalks that end in huge, two-inch-deep, violet flowers. Each flower only remains open until noon. Available from reputable growers. Do not collect from its native habitat.

Blanket flower (*Gaillardia grandiflora*)
Zones 8–11. Height: 6–24". Tough flowering plant that withstands the worst heat, salt, and drought conditions Florida has to offer. Often found growing wild alongside roads and on dunes. Daisy-like red and yellow blooms year-round. Will re-seed itself, but is not aggressive. Attracts butterflies. Grow from seed or bedding plants.

Century plant (*Agave americana*)
Zones 9–11. Height: 1–20'. Rosettes of fleshy, stiff leaves that can be up to six feet in diameter, with bloom clusters capable of attaining heights of twenty feet. There are more than three hundred *Agave* species, and they include some of Florida's best landscape plants, with sculptural qualities, dramatic color and forms, and excellent heat, salt, and drought tolerance. Grow in full sun for best performance. (See Plate 18.)

Coontie (*Zamia floridana*)
Zones 8–11. Height: 3'. Coontie is a cycad, an ancient fern or palm-like plant with evergreen, leathery fronds and palm-like growth habits. Often called a coontie palm. Grows in full sun to shade and prefers well-drained soils. Excellent choice for its sculptural quality and slow growth.

Coral bean, pink-flowered variety (*Erythrina herbacea*)
Zones 8–10. Height: 3'. The top half of each of this plant's flowering stems is lined with dozens of pink, tubular flowers. After flowering, slightly prickly branches clothed with trifoliate (three leaflets), pea-like foliage emerge. Grow in full to partial sun. Also recommended is the *Erythrina x bidwillii* hybrid coral bean, which grows to six feet and produces twenty-inch-long, arching spires of bright-red, tubular flowers.

Coreopsis or tickseed (*Coreopsis* spp.)
Zones 8–11. Height: 1–3'. Profusions of sunny yellow, two- to three-inch, daisy-like blooms distinguish this heat- and drought-tolerant plant. Grow from seed or bedding plants. There are several native varieties including *Coreopsis helianthoides*, swamp tickseed, and *Coreopsis integrifolia*, or Chipola River tickseed.

Crinum lily, string lily, or swamp lily (*Crinum americanum*)
Zones 8–11. Height: 3–5'. Flowering bulbs with clusters of fragrant, white, trumpet-shaped blooms on spikes that range from two to four feet above green, strap-like

foliage. Sun with some shade is preferred. *Crinum americanum* is native to the Panhandle, and grows to twenty inches with clusters of fragrant, white, star-shaped blooms.

Gama grass, Florida dwarf grass, or Fakahatchee grass (*Tripsacum floridanum*)
Zones 9–11. Height: 2–3'. Lush clumps of long, arching blades best grown in shaded, moist locations. Produces slender spikes of small red flowers. Dwarf gamma grass is a more compact plant.

Leather fern (*Acrostichum danaeifolium*)
Zones 9–11. Height: 6–10'. Handsome, very large, shrubby fern with a five- to ten-foot spread. Has a lush tropical appearance and is best grown in brackish or fresh-water marshes or otherwise wet soil in partial shade.

Louisiana iris (*Iris* spp.)
Zones 8–10. Height: 2–3'. Hardy, the heat- and humidity-tolerant iris is great for Florida gardens. The blue flag variety has deep-blue, dramatic blooms in spring and early summer. Good for wet areas and water gardens and available in all the colors of the rainbow. Can tolerate some shade.

Milkweed (*Asclepias* spp.)
Zones 8–10. Height: 1–3'. Deep-orange to red-and-yellow flower clusters. Perennial in most areas, and attractive to butterflies (especially monarchs), hummingbirds, and bees. *Asclepias incarnata* has fragrant red blooms.

Rain lily or fairy or zephyr lily (*Zephyranthes atamasco, Zephyranthes treatiae,* and *Zephyranthes simpsoni*)
Zones 8–10. Height: 1'. Bulbs produce white or pink flowers on stems extending up to a foot above strap-like foliage. Provide full sun and well-drained, rich soil. A wide range of nonnative rain lilies and hybrids from Mexico and Indonesia exist, with bloom colors including yellow, apricot, orange, and rose. Some have especially large blooms.

Scorpion-tail heliotrope or butterfly heliotrope (*Heliotropium angiospermum*)
Zones 9–11. Height: 1–3'. Mounded growth form with small white, lavender, or purple (*Heliotropium amplexicaule*) flower clusters. Can tolerate some shade and drought. Dies back in cooler areas. Attracts butterflies.

Tampa verbain (*Glandularia tampensis*)
Zones 9–11. Height: 1'. A verbena-like flowering plant with winter-blooming, lavender flowers that attract butterflies.

White star grass (*Dichromena latifolia*)
Zones 8–10. Height: 15–45". Slowly spreading clumps (at the rate of three feet in

two years) of green foliage with fifteen-inch stalks topped with spectacular white bracts (modified leaves) surrounding tiny flowers. Prefers a moist, boggy site, but will grow in all but the driest of sites.

Yucca (*Yucca filamentosa*)
Zones 8–11. Height: 2–5'. Large genus of fleshy-leaved plants that are famously heat and drought tolerant. All require good drainage and full sun. 'Golden Sword' variety has bright-yellow foliage with green margins, while 'Bright Edge' has narrow, dark-green leaves edged with a wide band of creamy gold.

Vines

Clematis (*Clematis crispa*)
Zones 8–11. Length: 2–8'. Evergreen vine which produces one- to two-inch white "bells" with recurved petals that show purple underneath. (See Plate 32.)

Trumpet vine (*Campsis radicans*)
Zones 8–10. Length: 20'+. Deciduous vine with clusters of showy, orange-red trumpets in summer. Requires substantial support and partial shade. (See Plate 14.)

Shrubs

Azalea or Florida flame (*Rhododendron austrinum* and Pinxter azalea *Rhododendron canescens*)
Zones 8–9. Height: 8–10'+. Both deciduous, rangy shrubs. Florida flame has clusters of brilliant yellow-orange blooms and Pinxter has clusters of fragrant pink/white blooms. Shallow-rooted, these acid-lowing plants prosper in well-drained, acidic soils provided they receive adequate moisture and midday shade. Drought tolerant once established.

Florida anise (*Illicium floridanum*)
Zones 8–10. Height: 5–20'. Native shrub or small tree with glossy evergreen foliage and dense, compact growth that exudes a distinct licorice fragrance. Grow in shade to full sun.

Florida boxwood (*Schaefferia frutescens*)
Zones 10–11. Height: 4–25'. Can be maintained as an evergreen shrub or allowed to become a small tree. Salt tolerant and thrives in rocky, alkaline soil. Insignificant flowers are produced early in the rainy season and are followed by clusters of little red berries that are attractive to wildlife.

Florida privet (*Forestiera segregata*)
Zones 8–11. Height: 15'. Evergreen, compact shrub with fine foliage, clusters of small yellow blooms, and small, olive-like fruits that are attractive to wildlife.

Gallberry (*Ilex glabra*)
Zones 8–11. Height: 10'. Large, loose, evergreen shrub suitable for full sun or partial shade that provides food for wildlife.

Golden dewdrop (*Duranta erecta*)
Zones 9–11. Height: 4–6'. Upright growth habit with heads of small single flowers in blue, white, purple, and variegated, depending on variety. Blooms are followed by yellow berries that provide food for wildlife. Dwarf varieties have a more compact growth habit. Attracts butterflies, hummingbirds, and other birds.

Needle palm (*Rhapidophyllum hystrix*)
Zones 8–11. Height: 8'. Thick, clump-forming palm with delicate, evergreen fronds. Drought tolerant. Partial shade preferred.

Oakleaf hydrangea (*Hydrangea quercifolia*)
Zones 8–9. Height: 4–15'. Loose, spreading growth habit, large, oak-like leaves, and showy, one-foot spikes of creamy blooms in early summer. Rich, red-bronze fall color on a deciduous shrub. Partial shade and rich, well-drained soil preferred.

Palmetto (*Sabal minor*)
Zones 8–11. Height: 4'. Small, slow-growing palm good for naturalized areas. Full sun to partial shade preferred. Tolerant of drought, heat, and humidity once established. The several available varieties include 'Bear Creek,' 'Blountstown Dwarf,' 'Castor Dwarf,' 'Savannah Silver,' 'Woodville,' and 'Sonoran Palmetto.'

Red cedar (*Juniperus virginiana*)
Zones 8–9. Height: 8'. When trimmed as a hedge, red cedar provides a thick wall of fine evergreen foliage that offers both cover and nesting sites for birds. Useful as a drought- and heat-tolerant tree.

Silver buttonwood (*Conocarpus erectus* variation *sericeus*)
Zones 10–11. Height: 4–20'. Often used as a shrub, but it can also be maintained as a small tree. Handsome, silver, felt-like foliage is evergreen. Very salt, drought, and heat tolerant. Tolerates wet or dry conditions and prefers full sun.

Sweetshrub (*Calycanthus floridus*)
Zones 8–9. Height: 6–10'. Glossy, dark-green leaves and fragrant, two-inch, ma-

roon spring blooms distinguish this deciduous native. Colorful yellow foliage in fall. Best for moist, shaded areas. Hybrid 'Hartlage Wine' (*Calycanthus* x *raulstonii*) has four-inch, non-fragrant blooms, and 'Venus' (*Calycanthus x venus*) offers large, magnolia-like blooms in early summer that have a powerful fragrance of strawberries, melons, and spices.

Saw palmetto (*Serenoa repens*)
Zones 8–11. Height: 6'. Clump-forming evergreen palm that grows in all sun and soil conditions. Very salt tolerant. Its flowers are attractive to bees, its fruits provide food for wildlife, and its foliage provides habitat.

Virginia willow or sweetspire (*Itea virginica*)
Zones 8–9. Height: 3'. Compact, mounded shrub with dramatic, long spikes of pure-white blooms and brilliantly red fall foliage. Prefers moist soils and shaded locations.

Yaupon holly (*Ilex vomitoria*)
Zones 8–10. Height: 1–20'. The epitome of a well-mannered shrub, this hardy native plant offers dense foliage, fine evergreen leaves, and slow growth along

Yaupon holly (*Ilex vomitoria*) is a valuable evergreen shrub with fine foliage that can be trimmed into various shapes.

with excellent heat, salt, and drought tolerance once it is established. It is one of the best small shrubs to be found, and takes well to trimming, even topiary. Produces small red berries that are attractive to wildlife. Can also be grown as a small tree.

Trees

Buttonbush (*Cephalanthus occidentalis*)
Zones 8–11. Height: 6–20'. Shrubby tree suited for shaded, wet sites that produces attractive, fuzzy, ball-like, two-inch blooms in the summer that attract butterflies and bees. Look for 'Sputnik,' a variety with large flowers and a long bloom time.

Cocoplum (*Chrysobalanus icaco*)
Zones 10–11. Height: 10–20'. Very dense shrub or small tree with waxy evergreen foliage and tiny white blooms year-round. Produces small, edible fruits good for jelly and wildlife. Excellent salt tolerance.

Dahoon (*Ilex cassine*)
Zones 8–11. Height: 40'. Evergreen holly with a narrow, upright growth habit that is suitable for wet and shaded locations and provides bright-red berries in winter, offering food and habitat to wildlife.

Dogwood (*Cornus florida*)
Zones 8–9. Height: 15–40'. Attractive, dense spring flowers and an appealing, spreading form are characteristics of this native plant. Relatively slow growing. Produces clusters of red fruit enjoyed by various bird species. A related species, swamp dogwood (*Cornus foemina*), has tiny, white, springtime blooms, a more shrubby growth habit (grows to about twenty-five feet), and is suitable for moist areas in Zones 8–9.

Fiddlewood (*Citharexylum fruticosum*)
Zone 11. Height: 25'. Evergreen, shrubby small tree with small, year-round, fragrant white blooms that produce dark drupes attractive to wildlife.

Florida thatch palm or Caribbean thatch palm (*Thrinax radiata*)
Zones 10–11. Height: 30'. Erect, fast-growing palm best grown in full sun. Somewhat cold tolerant.

Florida yew (*Taxus floridana*)
Zones 8–9. Height: 20'. A shrubby, rare, evergreen tree with spruce-like foliage. Limited to use in the Florida Panhandle.

Fringe tree (*Chionanthus virginicus*)
Zones 8–10. Height: 15–30'. Highly prized, graceful tree with a springtime display

of creamy, fragrant, fringe-like blooms that are followed by drooping clusters of dark fruit. Very drought tolerant.

Geiger tree (*Cordia sebestena*)
Zones 10–11. Height: 10–30'. Showy clusters of brilliant-red to orange trumpet-shaped blooms and large, heart-shaped leaves on a well-rounded, small tree make this one of the best flowering native trees. Salt and drought tolerant.

Hawthorn (*Crataegus* spp.)
Zones 8–10. Height: 25'. Small, deciduous tree with delicate foliage and numerous white or pink spring apple blossom blooms and edible fruits. Good for light shade and woodland plantings.

Hornbeam or blue beech or musclewood (*Carpinus caroliniana*)
Zones 8–9. Height: 30'. Slow-growing tree with interesting, bluish-gray bark and attractive springtime catkin blooms. Suited for moist, shaded locations. Tolerates occasional flooding. Provides food for tiger swallowtail and red-spotted purple butterfly larvae as well as other wildlife.

Jamaica caper (*Capparis cynophallophora*)
Zones 10–11. Height: 15–18'. Dense, evergreen, compact shrub or small tree suited for well-drained soils and full sun to partial shade. Very salt tolerant. Waxy, deep-green leaves and brush-like, white/purple blooms throughout spring and summer distinguish this exceptional plant.

Lignum vitae (*Guaiacum sanctum*)
Zones 10–11. Height: 10–30'. Clusters of gorgeous blue blooms in late spring and sporadically through summer on an evergreen tree. A protected species. Very slow growing and salt tolerant. Its extremely hard wood has long been revered by ship-builders.

Pawpaw (*Asimina obovata*)
Zones 8–10. Height: 5–30'. Small deciduous tree with large leaves and showy, drooping, creamy blooms in early spring. The tree is host to zebra swallowtail butterfly larvae. Drought and heat tolerant.

Red buckeye (*Aesculus pavia*)
Zones 8–9. Height: 6–25'. Small understory tree adaptable to shaded locations, either moist or dry. Magnificent sprays of red flowers in early spring are attractive to hummingbirds and butterflies, as are the golden-brown fruits to wildlife. Cold hardy.

Sea grape (*Coccoloba uvifera*)
Zones 9–11. Height: 3–35'. As a large shrub or tree, the sea grape is unequalled for its drought and salt tolerance. Handsome leathery leaves on a multibranched tree. It also makes for an excellent container specimen when small. Produces tiny white flowers year-round, followed by attractive, grape-like clusters of edible, one-inch fruits that can be used for jelly or as food for wildlife.

Silver palm (*Coccothrinax argentata*)
Zones 10–11. Height: 5–20'. Delicate, silvery fronds and a short, erect growth pattern. Very slow-growing and long-lived. Showy clusters of flowers and fruits tempt wildlife. Very drought and salt tolerant.

Simpson's stopper (*Myrcianthes fragrans*)
Zones 8–11. Height: 25'. Aromatic foliage smelling of nutmeg, showy, fragrant white blooms, and orange berries attractive to wildlife distinguish this plant. Tolerates a range of soil and sun conditions and is salt tolerant.

Spicewood (*Calyptranthes pallens*)
Zones 10–11. Height: 20'. Attractive, large, dense shrub or small tree with fragrant and colorful evergreen foliage. Small red to purple berries are attractive to wildlife. Prefers moist but well-drained soil and shaded locations.

Wax myrtle (*Myrica cerifera*)
Zones 8–11. Height: 25'. Fine, aromatic evergreen foliage with a loose, sprawling growth habit. Provides small waxy drupes that are attractive to wildlife and can be used in "bayberry" candle-making. Tolerates shade well.

Wild cinnamon (*Canella winterana*)
Zone 11. Height: 15–25'. Evergreen tree with an upright growth habit, fragrant bark, and leathery, dark-green leaves. Produces purple, red, or violet flowers in fall and winter, followed by fruits which wild birds enjoy. Excellent heat, drought, and salt tolerance.

Yellow elder (*Tecoma stans*)
Zones 10–11. Height: 15'. Small, evergreen tree with clusters of showy, two-inch, yellow flowers on new growth. Full sun is preferred.

Appendix

Aggressive and Rampant Plants to Avoid

Common names are included here as many new or casual gardeners may find them more recognizable. Please note that some of the following plants are not considered invasive everywhere in Florida, and some cultivars are valuable additions to the garden.* Though many of the following plants, shrubs, and trees are attractive in their own right, all are aggressive, and many are invasive. Consider yourself warned.

Asparagus fern *Asparagus sprengeri*
Australian pine *Casuarina* spp.
Brazilian pepper *Schinus terebinthifolius*
Cajeput tree *Melaleuca viridiflora*
Camphor tree *Cinnamomum camphora*
Canna *Cannaceae* spp.
Cashmere bouquet *Clerodendrum bungei*
Cat-claw vine *Macfadyena unguis-cati*
Chinaberry *Melia azedarach*
Chinese glory bower *Clerodendrum chinensis*
Coral honeysuckle *Lonicera sempervirens*
Coral vine *Antigonon leptopus*
Downy myrtle *Rhodomyrtus tomentosa*
Dwarf poinciana *Sesbania (Daubentonia) punicea*
Elephant ear *Colocasia* spp.
False banyan *Ficus altissima*
Four-o'-clock *Mirabilis jalapa*
Glossy privet *Ligustrum lucidum*
Golden rain tree *Koelreuteria elegans*
Guava *Psidium* spp.
Heavenly bamboo *Nandina domestica*
Japanese honeysuckle *Lonicera japonica*
Lantana *Lantana camara*
Mahoe *Hibiscus tileaceus*

Mexican petunia *Ruellia tweediana*
Mimosa or woman's-tongue tree *Albizia* spp.
Morning glory *Ipomoea* spp.
Orchid tree *Bauhinia variegata*
Oyster plant *Tradescantia spathacea*
Plumbago *Plumbago auriculata*
Portia tree *Thespesia populnea*
Pothos *Epipremnum pinnatum 'Aureum'*
Purple heart or purple queen *Tradescantia pallida*
Queen palm *Syagrus romanzoffianum*
Red firespike *Odontonema cuspidatum*
Red passionflower *Passiflora coccinea*
Rice paper plant *Tetrapanax* spp.
Sapodilla *Manilkara zapota*
Schefflera *Schefflera actinophylla*
Senegal date palm *Phoenix reclinata*
Silverthorn *Elaeagnus pungens*
Spanish bayonet *Yucca aloifolia*
Surinam cherry *Eugenia uniflora*
Sword fern or narrow sword fern *Nephrolepis cordifolia/multiflora/cordata*
Toog *Bischofia javanica*
Tropical almond *Terminalia* spp.
Wedelia *Wedelia trilobata*
Wisteria *Wisteria sinensis*

*Remember that "aggressive" and "invasive" don't mean the same thing. A Florida invasive plant is one that has been officially classified as such by the Florida Exotic Pest Plant Council (FLEPPC) because it has been proven to outcompete native plants and to damage native ecosystems. It is against the law to transport or sell many species of invasive plants.

Glossary

annual: a plant which produces foliage, blooms, and seeds, then dies, all in the course of one growing season

berry: small, fleshy fruit with one or more seeds

biennial: plant which produces foliage its first growing season, blooms, produces seeds, then dies in its second growing season

blight: a category of diseases that destroy plants and prevent growth

bole: the main trunk and extended unbranched stem

bract: a modified leaf that is technically not part of a flower though it may develop flower-like color

bulb: a thick, generally subterranean stem bud

clumping: a slow type of plant growth wherein the organism is limited to a clump

compost: decomposed organic matter comprised of formerly living organisms

corm: a small, bulblike, underground part of a plant such as a gladiolus

creeping: a horizontal, low-growth habit that produces sideways foliage and roots

crown: the leafy canopy of a tree, containing its principal foliage

crown-shaft: the extended bole in palm and palm-like trees

cultivar: a variety of plant of which all types were obtained asexually from one plant species

cuttings: portions of plant limbs or stems often used to produce new plants by inducing root formation

deadhead: to remove spent blossoms to prolong bloom time

deciduous: plant which annually sheds its leaves for a period of dormancy

determinate: a descriptor of plants with fixed growth limits, often referring to tomato plants suitable for container culture

division/dividing: breaking, slicing, or pulling a plant into more than one independent organism

dormancy: a period of time in which a plant is not actively growing or expanding

double: a flower with more than one complement of petals

drip line: the circular area around a plant determined by the circumference of its outermost limbs/foliage

drupe: a fleshy seed or fruit with one seed

dwarf: a miniature version of a full-sized plant

epiphyte/epiphytic: a plant which grows on a host plant for support but is not actively parasitic

evergreen: a plant that retains its leaves year-round

exotic: a plant which is not native to an area or habitat but is not necessarily invasive unless classified as such

fleshy: moisture-storing, juicy

forcing: to hasten growth by artificial methods, such as pre-cooling flowering bulbs

fungicide: a chemical toxin designed to kill fungus

graft: to splice a bud onto a particular rootstock

ground cover: plantings which grow horizontally or in a low, spreading manner that covers the ground

habit, also growth habit: the growth pattern or the way a particular plant normally grows

habitat: the location where a particular plant grows

hardiness zones: cold-hardiness zones are areas in which specific plants are deemed able to survive the typical cold, and measure the lowest temperatures that can be expected in an average year, as determined by the United States Department of Agriculture

heat zones: heat-hardiness zones are areas in which specific plants can grow or survive the heat, and measure the average number of days with temperatures over eighty-six degrees Fahrenheit that occur each year, as determined by the American Horticultural Society

herbaceous: a plant lacking woody tissue which often dies or goes dormant at the end of its growing season

herbicide: a chemical toxin designed to kill undesirable plants

hybrid: a plant created from the cross-breeding of two genetically dissimilar species

indeterminate: a descriptor of plants lacking growth limits, often referring to tomato plants (see "determinate" above)

indigenous: a plant native to a particular area

insecticide: a chemical toxin designed to kill insects

invasive: a plant which grows uncontrollably, crowding out native plants

medium: the material in which plants, seeds, cuttings, and so forth are grown, a substrate which supplies nutrients and support

monoculture: a species that grows (or is cultivated) to the exclusion of all others at the expense of biodiversity

mulch: a porous material used to cover the ground surrounding plants

native: a plant which occurs in a particular area

nematode: a harmful microscopic organism naturally existing in soil that attacks roots; note that beneficial nematodes also exist

nutrient: a compound or element necessary for plant growth, such as nitrogen or phosphorous

organic: any fertilizer, mulch, pesticide, herbicide, fungicide, or other compound derived from plants or animals

panicle: a branch of flowers (inflorescence or cluster), for example those which occur on crape myrtles

perennial: an herbaceous plant which continues to live year after year, oftentimes experiencing a dormant period during the coldest portion of the year

pest: any organism, including insects, animals, fungus, and bacteria, that is directly or indirectly harmful to plants

pollen: dust-like grains which are the male gametes of flowering plants (angiosperms)

pollinator: insects, birds, bats, or other organisms which transfer pollen to the receptive organ in a plant's flower, thereby fertilizing it and allowing the plant to produce fruit/seeds

rhizome: a horizontally growing, swollen end portion of a stem which spreads by producing roots and shoots

rosette: a whorl of leaves or petals around a central point, as in a bromeliad

seedling: a small plant grown from seed

shrub: a woody plant with branches near its base

specimen: an especially showy plant that is given center stage in landscape design

standard: a plant, often a shrub, with growth restricted to one straight, erect stem from which a number of limbs are allowed to grow in a compact pattern at the top of the main stem to resemble a small tree

subtropical: a climatic region existing north of the tropical region and characterized by slightly colder weather

sucker: a fleshy, auxiliary shoot emanating from the root, trunk, or stalk of a plant

terrestrial: plants which grow in the ground, rather than in water or air

tuber: a swollen, fleshy, underground portion of a plant from which new shoots sprout

vine: a climbing plant

volunteer: a plant that is self-seeded by a parent plant rather than intentionally planted by the gardener

Sources and Resources

Seeds, Bulbs, Plants, and Gardening Supplies Available
Online and by Mail Order

Back Saver Grip (ergonomic tool conversion): MBS, Inc., 3511 West Green Tree
Road, Milwaukee, WI 53209; 1-800-752-7874 (www.backsavergrip.com)

Baker Creek Heirloom Seeds (Seminole pumpkin and other rare seeds): 2278 Baker
Creek Road, Mansfield, MO 65704; 1-417-924-8887 (www.rareseeds.com)

Bradfield Organics (organic fertilizers for lawn and garden): 555 Maryville University Drive, St. Louis, MO 63141; 1-800-551-9564 (www.bradfieldorganics.com)

Casco Bay Gardens, LLC (Lobsterman's Silicone Balm): 1776 Broadway, South Portland, ME 04106; 1-207-773-9129 (www.lbalm.com)

Dyna-Gro Nutrition Solutions (plant fertilizers and root-stimulating products):
2775 Giant Road, Richmond, CA 94806; 1-800-396-2476 (www.dyna-gro.com)

Fish in the Garden (stoneware garden ornamentation): 1-207-797-2988 (www.
FishInTheGarden.com)

Hydrolysate Company of America (MultiBloom and MegaGreen catfish-based organic fertilizers): P.O. Box 271, Iola, MS 38754; 1-662-962-3101 (www.multibloom.
com)

Johnny Selected Seeds: 955 Benton Avenue, Winslow, ME 04901; 1-800-564-6697
(www.johnnyseeds.com)

JRM Chemical, Inc. (Soil Moist mycorrhizal products): 4881 Northeast Parkway,
Cleveland, OH 44128; 1-800-962-4010 (www.soilmoist.com)

Klehm's Song Sparrow Perennial Farm: 13101 East Rye Road, Avalon, WI 53505; 1-800-553-3715 (www.songsparrow.com)

Monterey Lawn & Garden Products, Inc. (organic herbicides, fungicides, insecticides, molluscicides, rodenticides, growth regulators, fertilizers, adjuvants, and repellents): P.O. Box 35000, Fresno, CA 93745; 1-559-499-2100 (www.monterey lawngarden.com)

Old House Gardens (heirloom bulbs): 536 Third Street, Ann Arbor, MI 48103; 1-734-995-1486 (www.oldhousegardens.com)

Plant Delights Nursery: 9241 Sauls Road, Raleigh, NC 27603; 1-919-772-4794 (www.plantdelights.com)

Proven Winners (annuals, perennials, shrubs, vines, and trees): 111 East Elm Street, Suite D, Sycamore, IL 60178; 1-877-865-5818 (www.provenwinners.com)

Renee's Garden Seeds: 6116 Highway 9, Felton, CA 95018 (www.reneesgarden. com)

Richters Herb Specialists: 357 Highway 47, Goodwood, Ontario, LOC 1AD Canada; 1-905-640-6677 (www.richters.com)

Seeds of Change: P.O. Box 15700, Santa Fe, NM 87592; 1-888-762-7333 (www.seeds ofchange.com)

Spray-N-Grow (organic sprays and fertilizers): P.O. Box 2137, Rockport, TX 78381; 1-800-323-2363 (www.spray-n-grow.com)

Stokes Tropicals: P.O. Box 9868, New Iberia, LA 70562; 1-800-624-9706 (www. stokestropicals.com)

Territorial Seeds: P.O. Box 158, Cottage Grove, OR 97424; 1-800-626-0866 (www. territorialseed.com)

The Southern Bulb Co.: P.O. Box 350, Golden, TX 75444; 1-903-768-2530 (www. southernbulbs.com)

Whiteflower Farm: P.O. Box 50, Litchfield, CT 06759; 1-800-503-9624 (www.white flowerfarm.com)

Gardening Associations

American Horticultural Society: 7931 East Boulevard Drive, Alexandria, VA 22308; 1-703-768-5700 or 1-800-777-7931 (www.ahs.org or, to view their heat zone map, visit: www.ahs.org/pdfs/05_heat_map.pdf)

American Orchid Society: 16700 AOS Lane, Delray Beach, FL 33446; 1-561-404-2000 (www.aos.org)

Association of Florida Native Nurseries: P.O. Box 434, Melrose, FL 32666; 1-321-917-1960 (www.afnn.org)

Florida-Georgia Iris Society (Louisiana iris): P.O. Box 41, Woodbine, GA 31569

Florida Gourd Society, Inc.: (www.flgourdsoc.org)

Florida Native Plant Society: P.O. Box 278, Melbourne, FL 32902 (www.fnps.org)

Florida Nursery, Growers, and Landscape Association: 1533 Park Center Drive, Orlando, FL 32835 (www.fngla.org)

Florida State Beekeepers Association: (www.floridabeekeepers.org)

International Water Lily and Water Gardening Society: 6828 26th Street West, Bradenton, FL 34207; 1-941-756-0880 (www.iwgs.org)

Plant a Row for the Hungry, Garden Writers Association: 10210 Leatherleaf Court, Manassas, VA 20111; 1-877-492-2727 (www.gardenwriters.org)

Acknowledgments

Any book is a process, and most vital to this one has been the steady hand of John Byram, who provided both inspiration and guidance. The eagle eyes, expertise, and experience of Kim Taylor, Tom MacCubbin, and the ever-precise Corey Brady have been invaluable to this project, keeping me on my toes and accurate. Resourceful Kara Schwartz and Michele Fiyak-Burkley have come to my rescue more than once. But above all, I would like to acknowledge my husband, Bob, who time and again helped to make sure that everything that needed to be said and done was. Thank you all.

Bibliography

American Horticultural Society. *AHS Great Plant Guide*. New York: DK Publishing, Inc., 1999.

Appell, Scott D. (editor). *Annuals for Every Garden: Brooklyn Botanic Garden All-Region Guide*. New York: Brooklyn Botanic Garden, Inc., 2003.

Armitage, Alan M. *Armitage's Manual of Annuals, Biennials, and Half-Hardy Perennials*. Portland, Ore.: Timber Press, 2001.

Bartlett, R. D., and Patricia Bartlett. *Florida's Snakes: A Guide to Their Identification and Habits*. Gainesville, Fla.: University Press of Florida, 2003.

Brown, Sydney Park, and Rick K. Schoellhorn. *Your Florida Guide to Perennials*. Gainesville, Fla.: University Press of Florida, 2006.

Coombes, Allen J. *Dictionary of Plant Names*. Portland, Ore.: Timber Press, 1997.

Cutler, Karen Davis. *Pruning Trees, Shrubs and Vines: Brooklyn Botanic Garden All-Region Guide*. New York: Brooklyn Botanic Garden, Inc., 2003.

Dirr, Michael A. *Dirr's Trees and Shrubs for Warm Climates: An Illustrated Encyclopedia*. Portland, Ore.: Timber Press, 2002.

Florida Water Management Districts. *Waterwise Florida Landscapes, 2nd Edition*. February 2003.

Foote, Leonard E., and Samuel B. Jones Jr. *Native Shrubs and Woody Vines of the Southeast: Landscape Uses and Identification*. Portland, Ore.: Timber Press, 1998.

Garden Club of Palm Beach. *Gardens by the Sea: Creating a Tropical Paradise*. Gainesville, Fla.: University Press of Florida, 1999.

Gillman, Jeff. *The Truth About Organic Gardening: Benefits, Drawbacks, and the Bottom Line*. Portland, Ore.: Timber Press, 2008.

Grey-Wilson, Christopher, and Victoria Matthews. *Gardening with Climbers*. Portland, Ore.: Timber Press, 1997.

Hannermann, Monika, Patricia Hulse, Brian Johnson, Barbara Kurland, and Tracey Patterson. *Gardening with Children*. New York: Brooklyn Botanic Garden, Inc., 2007.

Llamas, Kirsten Albrecht. *Tropical Flowering Plants: A Guide to Identification and Cultivation*. Portland, Ore.: Timber Press, 2003.

MacCubbin, Tom. *The Edible Landscape, Revised Edition*. Oviedo, Fla.: Waterview Press, 1998.

Mackey, Betty Barr, and Monica Moran Brandies. *A Cutting Garden for Florida, 3rd Edition*. Wayne, Penn.: B. B. Mackey Books, 2001.

Nelson, Gil. *Florida's Best Native Landscape Plants: 200 Readily Available Species for Homeowners and Professionals*. Gainesville, Fla.: University Press of Florida, 2003.

Ortho Books staff. *All About Citrus & Subtropical Fruits*. San Francisco, Calif.: Ortho Books, 1985.

Osorio, Rufino. *A Gardener's Guide to Florida Native Plants*. Gainesville, Fla.: University Press of Florida, 2001.

Rice, Graham. *Discovering Annuals*. Portland, Ore.: Timber Press, 1999.

Riffle, Robert Lee. *The Tropical Look: An Encyclopedia of Dramatic Landscape Plants*. Portland, Ore.: Timber Press, 1998.

Stearn, William T. *Stearn's Dictionary of Plant Names for Gardeners*. Portland, Ore.: Timber Press, 2002.

Steens, Andrew. *Bromeliads for the Contemporary Garden*. Portland, Ore.: Timber Press, 2003.

Watkins, John V., Thomas J. Sheehan, and Robert J. Black. *Florida Landscape Plants: Native and Exotic, 2nd Revised Edition*. Gainesville, Fla.: University Press of Florida, 2005.

Index

Fakahatchee grass. *See* gama grass

false banyan *Ficus altissima*, 161

false dragonhead (obedient plant) *Physotegia virginiana*, 124

false hydrangea vine *Schizophragma* spp., 138

false Queen Anne's lace (esp. 'Green Mist' and 'White Dill') *Ammi majus*, 114

false vervain. *See* porterweed

Farfugium japonicum leopard plant, 135

fava bean, 74

fencing gardens, electric, "invisible," and mesh, 51

fertilizers, understanding the numbers, 82

Ficus altissima false banyan, 161

fiddlewood *Citharexylum fruticosum*, 157

firebush *Hamelia patens*, 48

firecracker plant (coral plant) *Russelia equisetiformis*, 124

first-aid for gardeners, 52–55, plate 22

fishtail palm *Caryota mitis*, 147

flame vine *Pyrostegia venusta*, 138, plate 14

flamingo flower. *See* jacobinia

flamingo flowers. *See* anthurium

flax lily *Daniella tasmanica variegata*, 124

flax *Linum* spp., 114

Florida anise *Illicium floridanum*, 154

Florida boxwood *Schaefferia frutescens*, 154

Florida dwarf grass. *See* gama grass

Florida Gourd Society Inc., 84, 169

Florida privet *Forestiera segregata*, 155

Florida State Association of Beekeepers, 79, 169

Florida thatch palm *Thrinax radiata*, 157

Florida yew (torreya) *Taxus floridana*, 157

flowering maple *Abutilon* spp., 125

flowering tobacco. *See* nicotiana

Foeniculum vulgare bronze fennel, 112

forest bell bush *Mackaya bella*, 142

Forestiera segragata Florida privet, 155

Fortunella spp. kumquat, 148

four-o'clock *Mirabilis jalapa*, 161

foxtail fern *Asparagus meyeri*, 134

frangipani *Plumeria* spp., 148

freeze protection, 74

friendship plant. *See* aluminum plant

fringe tree *Chionanthus virginicus*, 157

Gaillardia grandiflora blanket flower, 152

Gaillardia spp. blanket flower, 111

gallberry *Ilex glabra*, 155

gama grass (Florida dwarf grass or Fakahatchee grass) *Tripsacum floridanum*, 153

garden fencing, 51

gardenia *Gardenia jasminoides*, 142

gaura (wand flowers or whirling butterflies) *Gaura lindheimeri*, 131

geiger tree *Cordia sebestena*, 158

geranium *Pelargonium* spp., 125, plate 1

ginger: *Alpinia* spp., 134; *Costus* spp., 134; *Curcuma* spp., 134; *Globba* spp., 134; *Hedychium* spp., 134; *Kaempferia* spp., 134, 136; *Zingiber* spp., 134

Glandularia tampensis Tampa verbain, 153

glossy privet *Ligustrum lucidum*, 161

golden dewdrop *Duranta erecta*, 155

golden plume *Schaueria flavicoma*, 134

golden raintree *Koelreuteria elegans*, 161

gourd, 84

grape holly *Mahonia* spp., 143

grape hyacinth *Muscari neglectum*, 125

growing zones, 13–15

Guaiacum sanctum lignum vitae, 158

guava *Psidium* spp., 161

Gulf Stream temperature impact, 14

Guzmania spp. *See* bromeliad

Hamelia patens firebush, 48

hand truck, 55, plate 22

hardy orchid *Calanthe* spp., 134

Hawaiian ribbon fern (ribbon fern) *Pteris cretica*, 129

hawthorn *Crataegus* spp., 158

heat zones, 13–14

heavenly bamboo *Nandina domestica*, 161

Hedychium spp. ginger, 134

heirloom rose *Rosa* spp., 20, 145

heirloom tomatoes, 91

Helianthus debilis beach sunflower, 111

Helianthus spp. sunflower, 118

Heliotropium angiospermum scorpion-tail heliotrope (butterfly heliotrope), 153

Hemerocallis spp. daylily, 124, plate 23

Hemigraphis spp. red flame ivy (dragon's breath or waffle plant), 136

Heptacodium miconioides seven-son flower, 150

herbs, project, 56–58

hibiscus *Hibiscus rosa-sinensis*, 143

Hibiscus tileaceus mahoe, 161

Hippeastrum spp. amaryllis, 121

holly fern *Cyrtomium falcatum*, 135

hollyhock *Alcea rosea*, growing from seed, 17–18

honey bees, 78–79

honey flower *Melianthus major*, 143

honeywort. *See* cerinthe

hornbeam (blue beech or musclewood) *Carpinus caroliniana*, 158

horsemint *Monarda punctata*, 114

hummingbirds, flowers that attract, 48, 76

hurricane lily. *See* lycoris

hybrid rose *Rosa* spp., 145

Lynette L. Walther is the recipient of the National Garden Bureau's Exemplary Journalism Award and the Florida Magazine Association's Silver Award of Writing Excellence. She is a member of the Garden Writers Association and writes gardening-related columns for newspapers and magazines in Florida, where she gardens in the winter months, traveling to Maine for the summer.